Symbolic Logic

Fifth Edition
Revised

Daniel R. Kern, Ph.D.

Lexi Beck

Copyright 2021

978-1-716-44318-3
Imprint: Lulu.com

Contents

Chapter 1: Introductory Concepts

1.1 – Logic and Arguments

Logic is the study of argument. Another way of saying this is that logic is the study of human reasoning. The characteristic that is most often associated with how humans differ from other animals is that humans reason, while other animals don't.[1] Reason is the capacity to come to conclusions based on the evaluation of evidence, or based on argument. So logic is a very important study. It is the study of what makes us distinctive creatures in the world.

1.2 – Arguments

In general, in defining terms, it is not very helpful to define a term with other terms that are themselves not well-defined. This is the case with defining "logic" in terms of "argument." So it will help to provide a definition of "argument." Informally, when we think of an argument, we think of people having a disagreement about something and voicing their opinions about what they think is the right or wrong answer. In addition to just voicing their opinions however, people in an argument must be trying to convince the other people that their opinion is the correct one. The attempt to persuade or convince is the essential feature of arguments. Informally, we can define an argument as **a situation in which someone is trying to persuade or convince someone else that something is true or false**. We can define "argument" more specifically, based on this informal definition. The formal definition of "argument" (the one used by logicians) **a set of statements that includes (at least one *premise*, one *conclusion*, and) an inference**. This definition will change slightly – we will remove the words in parentheses.

---

[1] There may be other beings that have reason. Classically, angels and God have reason. It is also possible that there are other beings in the universe that have reason. And many contemporary biologists claim that some animals have reason (i.e., dolphins, higher-order primates, etc.). Among the beings that we know for sure exist, however, humans are the only beings that reason in the way or at the level that humans do.

1.3 – Statements

We now, though, have another definition that includes some undefined terms (statement, premises, conclusion, inference), so we should define those terms as well. There are several definitions for "statement." The two simplest ones are **a sentence that is either true or false** and **a sentence that says something about the world**. For instance, the sentence, "The sky is blue" is a statement. It says something about the world, about the color of the sky, and it is either true or false (in this case it is true (at least for normally-sighted humans on a clear day!)). Statements may be more complex than this one. For instance, "The governor of California asked the state government to pass a resolution declaring stem cell research legitimate and establishing a fund to promote stem cell research." This sentence still says something about the world (an action of the governor's) and it is either true or false (either the governor asked the government to do this or he didn't). All statements, though, have these characteristics.

Not all sentences are statements; statements are a subgroup of sentences. There are 3 types of sentences that are not statements. **Questions** are sentences, but not statements. "Where is Chicago?" is a proper sentence, but it doesn't say anything about the world and it is neither true nor false. **Commands** are also sentences but not statements. "Get out of bed!" is a is a proper sentence, but it doesn't say anything about the world and it is neither true or false. It is just a command. Finally, expressions of emotion, sometimes referred to as "exclamations" are sentences but not statements. If I stub my toe and yell "Ouch!" I have expressed a sentence, a complete thought, but I have not said anything about the world and my expression is neither true nor false.

One important clarification about statements must be made. Although statements are either true or false, it is not necessary that we know whether a sentence is true or false to call it a statement. For instance, "There is life on other planets" is a statement, even though we don't know whether it is true or false. It is either true or false, either there is life on other planets or not; the state of our knowledge doesn't affect that fact. Similarly, "There is a large animal living in Loch Ness in Scotland" is a statement, even though we don't know whether it is true or false.

1.4 – Subjective and Objective Statements

Statements are themselves sometimes divided into categories. There are two different ways of dividing statements, which produces some interesting relationships and is the basis of much philosophical discussion. The first division is between objective and subjective statements. An **objective statement** is one that says something about the world independent of the speaker's own beliefs, frame of mind, mental states, etc. "The sky is blue" is an example of an objective statement, as is "There is life on other planets" and "The square root of 4 is 2." These statements are either true or false independently of whether any person *thinks* they are true or false or even independently of whether any person *knows* they are true or false. A **subjective statement**, on the other hand, says something about the speaker's feelings, beliefs, states of mind, etc. For instance, "I am hungry," "I love Joe," and "I believe that Bill Clinton was a terrible president" are all subjective statements. It is important to note here that subjective statements meet the criterion for being statements. They say something about the world (in this case, the speaker's feelings, beliefs, etc.), and they are either true or false. For instance, if Joe says "I am hungry," we could determine whether it was true or false by watching Joe and seeing if he ate something (which would imply that his statement was true), or turned down some food that was offered to him (which would imply that his statement was false). If Mary says "I love Joe," we could ask Mary more about her feelings for Joe, to see if she really did love Joe, we could ask Joe if Mary loved him, we could ask other people that knew Mary and Joe if Mary seemed to love Joe, etc. So, although subjective statements are subjective (they deal with the speaker's feelings, beliefs, states of mind, etc.), and while it may be relatively difficult to determine whether they are true or false, they are still statements. What distinguishes subjective statements from objective statements is that a subjective statement may be true, if applied to one person, but false if applied to another. It is possible for Mary to say "I love Joe" and for it to be true, and at the same time for Sally to say "I love Joe" and for it to be false. This is because the truth of subjective statements depends on their connection to the person expressing them.

The other way of dividing up statements is between factual statements and value statements. A **factual** statement says something about the way the world *is*. "The sky is blue," and "Mary loves Joe" are both factual statements. A **value** statement, on the other hand, is a statement that places a **value** on something (or **evaluates** something). For instance, "We should end world hunger," "That painting is beautiful," and "Classical music is better than rock music" are all value statements. To evaluate something is not just to compare things. "Joe is taller than Bill" is a comparison, but is not an evaluation. Evaluation involves the implication that some states of things are better or more valuable than others. Any statement that involves evaluation is a value statement. There is a type of statement that can be misleading. If I say "I believe that we should end world hunger," I am not directly evaluating anything; I am directly talking about my beliefs. Hence, the statement is not a value statement, but a factual statement.

Given these two distinctions, it is an interesting question to wonder how they relate to each other. There are several possibilities, and we can use what is called a "square of opposition" to consider them.

	Subjective Statement	**Objective Statement**
Factual Statement	1	2
Value Statement	3	4

We now have 4 combinations. The first is statements that are subjective and factual. Statements such as "I like chocolate ice cream" and "I love the Dodgers" would go in this category. They are subjective statements, since they are about the speaker's feelings or beliefs. The second category is statements that are objective and factual. The vast majority of our statements falls into this category. Statements like "The sky is blue," "Mt. Saint Helens is in Washington State," "There is life on other planets," etc., are factual objective statements.

The third and fourth categories, dealing with value statements, are more complicated and more interesting. The third category is statements that are subjective and value statements. The majority of value statements fall into this category. "Chocolate ice cream is the best flavor" is a subjective value statement. It is a value statement because it evaluates ice cream. It is also subjective because most people who would make this claim would mean "*I think that* chocolate ice cream is the best flavor" and would not intend to say that chocolate ice cream should be held to be the best flavor by everyone. [2] All statements that express personal tastes fall into this category.

One of the most interesting questions in philosophy is the question of whether there are any statements that are both objective statements and value statements, or, whether there are any statements in category 4. That is, statements that propose to evaluate things on a basis that is not a matter of

---

[2] Technically, "I think that chocolate ice cream is the best" is an *objective* value statement; since it refers to a specific person it would be either true or false absolutely.

anyone's ideas or beliefs. There are two main possibilities for objective value statements: statements about beauty (aesthetic statements) and statements about morality. Some philosophers hold that there is an objective standard of beauty and that the statements "That picture is beautiful" and "That picture is ugly" (referring to some specific pictures) are true or false independently of whether any particular person believes them to be true or false, or even whether any person knows whether they are true or false. Similarly, many philosophers hold that the statement "We should end world hunger" is true whether any particular person believes it to be true. At the same time, there are many philosophers who argue that aesthetic statements are NOT objective, but subjective. They accept that "beauty is in the eye of the beholder." There are also philosophers that argue that moral statements are not objective, but subjective. This position is commonly known as "moral relativism," and is the belief that there are no objective moral values – the truth of any moral statement depends on whether the person stating it believes it to be true or not. I leave you to consider whether there are any statement that belong in category 4. One way of arguing that there are no objective value statements is not successful. That is, to say, "people don't agree about beauty or morality, so there must not be any objective standard" will not prove that value statements are not objective. For, we have already seen that "there is life on other planets" and "there is a Loch Ness monster" are objective statements, even though people don't agree about whether they are true or false. Furthermore, we have seen that statements (these, for instance) can be true or false even though we don't know the answer. So, the fact that people disagree about which pictures or music are beautiful or about which actions are right and wrong does not in itself mean that these value statements are not objective. But it doesn't prove that they are objective either...

Our chart may now be completed this way:

	Subjective Statement	**Objective Statement**
Factual Statement	**"I like chocolate ice cream"** **"I love Mary"** **etc.**	**"The sky is blue"** **"There is life on other planets"** **etc.**
Value Statement	**"Chocolate is the best flavor of ice cream"** **"The Los Angeles Padres are the best baseball team"** **etc.**	**"It is wrong to have an abortion" (?)** **"Van Gogh's *Starry Night* is a beautiful painting" (?)** **etc.**

Distinguishing Between Subjective and Objective Value Statements

Philosophers debate whether there are objective value statements. There is a criterion that may be used to help answer this question, and to distinguish between subjective and objective statements (although the criterion itself is debated). The criterion is this: **If people can have a *real argument* about a statement, the statement is objective, whether it is a subjective or objective statement.**

It is not entirely clear, on the surface, what a "*real* argument" is, so here is a criterion for identifying a "*real* argument." It appeals to our earlier definitions of "argument." A *real* argument is an argument in which someone is *really* trying to convince someone else that something is true. Now this may still not be entirely clear. An example may help. Two friends may have an "argument" about the statement, "Chocolate is the best flavor of ice cream." They may give reasons for their belief that it is or isn't the best flavor, they may accuse the other person of being incorrect in thinking chocolate is or isn't the best flavor, etc. But it is hard to imagine two people having a *real* argument, in which they are really trying to convince the other person that chocolate is or isn't the best flavor. So, although people can have play arguments about subjective value statements, they can't really have a *real* argument about them. However, consider the statement, "Abortion is morally okay." It is possible to have, and many people around the work are having, arguments about whether this statement is true or false. These are *real* arguments – the people in them are often working very hard to convince other people that the statement really is true or false (regardless of the fact that other people believe something different). This fact is a sign that the statement at issue is an objective statement. Now remember, statements can be objective even if people disagree about whether they are true or false, and even if people don't know whether they are true or false. Moral statements often fit into these categories. People clearly disagree about whether the statement "Abortion is morally okay" is true or false, and, given the extent of disagreement, it seems that we don't really know whether abortion is morally okay or not. But these facts don't necessarily make the statement subjective, just as they don't make the statement "There is life on other planets" subjective. According to this criterion, then, moral statements are objective value statements. However, it is to be noted that not all philosophers would accept this criterion and not all philosophers believe that moral statements are objective.

Aesthetic statements are difficult to determine even using this criterion. People do have arguments about whether certain paintings are beautiful or not, or "good art" or not, but it is not clear that these arguments are *real* arguments. So, even with this criterion, it is not clear whether aesthetic statements are objective or subjective (and there are people who think both).

1.5 – Premises and Conclusions

Returning to our definition, an argument is composed of statements. There are two types of statements in an argument that have a special relationship to each other. The ***premises*** of an argument are statements that give support or evidence for another statement. The ***conclusion*** of an argument is the statement that the premises give support or evidence for. For instance,

> *All students are humans.*
> *Bob is a student.*
> **Therefore, Bob is a human.**

The italicized statements, "All students are humans" and "Bob is a student," are the premises. They are taken to give support or evidence for the statement, "Bob is a human," which is the conclusion.

1.6 – Inference

The premises in an argument "support" and "infer"[3] the conclusion. These terms describe the relationship between the premises and the conclusion. That is, in an argument, if the premises are taken to be true, then the listener is somehow *motivated* or *influenced* to take the conclusion as true as well. This is a deep insight into human nature. This is what it means to say that humans are rational: we are naturally convinced by arguments in which the premises support the conclusion. We can't help but be persuaded by good arguments.[4]

The term "infer" is a Latin term, meaning "to carry in." This definition is helpful in understanding the sense of "infer" in arguments – the premises infer or "carry in" the conclusion. You can't let the premises in (as true) without letting the conclusion in (as true) along with them. Thus, the premises have a certain sort of relationship to the conclusion; namely, a

---

[3] Technically, premises imply and people infer. Since I am discussing inference here, I am purposely using the wrong term.

[4] Whether humans are always persuaded by good arguments is a matter of debate. Assuming that a person understands the argument, I argue that even though people might *act* as if they are unpersuaded by a good argument (due to emotions or some other influence), they are not in reality unpersuaded, they are just acting.

support relationship, or an **inferential** relationship. Our definition of "inference" will be **a relationship in which the truth of one or more statements (the premises) affects the probability of the truth of another statement (the conclusion).**

Types of Inference

Arguments are divided into categories depending on the type and strength of the support relationship between the premises and the conclusion. First, the premises can support the conclusion in an absolute way; that is, the truth of the premises guarantees the truth of the conclusion, absolutely. For instance, consider the argument already presented:

> All students are humans.
> Bob is a student
> Therefore, Bob is a human.

In this argument, if the premises are true (which we will assume for the moment), the conclusion MUST be true, it cannot be false. So we say the support relationship here is absolute. Arguments in which the support relationship is absolute are referred to as **DEDUCTIVE** arguments.

Now consider the argument:

> Most people who drive Jaguar cars are rich.
> Bob drives a Jaguar car.
> Therefore, Bob is rich.

In this argument, even if we take the premises to be true, there is no attempt to demonstrate absolutely that Bob is rich. The attempt is only to make the reader think it is *probable* that Bob is rich (the key here is the word "most" in the first premise). There is an attempt at persuasion here, but not in an absolute sense. An argument in which the premises only give *probabilistic* support for the conclusion (that is, they make the conclusion probably, not necessarily, true) are called **INDUCTIVE** arguments. Inductive arguments that make the conclusion very probable are better (more convincing) arguments, while inductive arguments that don't make the conclusion very probable are less convincing and worse arguments.

There is one more possible (but not very interesting) support relationship. That is, the premise could have nothing at all to do with the conclusion, in which case they don't really have a support relationship (that is, their truth has no effect on the probability of the truth of the conclusion. For instance,

The sky is blue.
Therefore, birds fly.

Although this text has the form of an argument, the premise has no support relationship with the conclusion, so this text is not properly an argument at all.

The different support relationships can be illustrated like this:

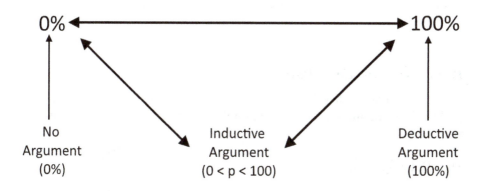

Strength of Support Relationships

1.7 – Identifying Arguments

Types of arguments

Arguments, then, fall into two categories. If the premises support the conclusion absolutely (the conclusion MUST be true if the premises are true), the argument is **deductive**. If the premises give a certain amount of probability to the conclusion (greater than 0, but less than 100% probability), the argument is **inductive**. Both inductive and deductive arguments are of interest to logicians, for different reasons. Deductive arguments are interesting because of the strength of the support relationship: the premises either prove the conclusion or they don't. Deductive arguments are either/or, and they show us a lot about how arguments and inferences work. We can learn a lot about what makes arguments good or bad from studying deductive arguments. Inductive arguments, on the other hand, are much more common than deductive arguments. Most of the arguments we encounter in everyday life are inductive, not deductive. So studying inductive arguments has a more directly practical application. In this course as a whole, we will be studying deductive arguments, and not inductive arguments, but it will be helpful to learn a little about recognizing and analyzing both deductive and inductive arguments to start.

We are already prepared to distinguish arguments from non-arguments. An argument is a text in which there is an attempt to persuade or convince someone of something. One method of identifying a passage as an argument it to ask whether the passage has a conclusion (something being argued for or supported). Once we have determined that a passage is an argument, the next task is to determine whether it is a deductive or inductive argument. This is not an easy task, and the easiest way to do it is to learn some typical argument patterns that identify arguments as deductive or inductive.

Inductive Argument Patterns

From our earlier discussion, we know that inductive arguments are probabilistic arguments. There are several common patterns of probabilistic arguments.

Statistical arguments

The most common type of inductive argument in our culture is the statistical argument, most commonly seen in polls. The following argument is a statistical argument:

> A Gallup poll revealed that 73% of Californians plan to vote in favor of Proposition 88, which will increase the strength of anti-smog regulations in Los Angeles county. Therefore, Proposition 88 will pass.

There is an attempt to persuade the reader that Proposition 88 will pass, but the attempt is not to *prove* that it will pass. The arguer is just announcing a probability that it will pass. There are a number of important issues in analyzing the strength of probabilistic arguments, but our task at this moment is just to identify them.

Causal Arguments

Another common type of inductive argument is the causal argument. A causal argument establishes a causal connection between 2 events, then establishes that the first event has happened, and concludes that the second event will also happen.

I left my car headlights on last night. Therefore, the battery will be dead this morning.

In this argument, the causal connection is well-known and assumed (leaving the headlights on in a car usually causes the battery to be dead the next morning). It is not necessary that the car battery will be dead (maybe this car has a very strong batter, etc). But it is probable. Technically, no matter how often a causal connection has occurred in the past, there is no guarantee that it will occur in the future (the world might end before it occurs). As a result, all causal arguments are inductive.

Analogies

Another very common inductive argument pattern is the analogy. In an analogy, a characteristic that applies to one object is said to apply to another object as well, based on similarities between the two:

> Mary is a national champion figure-skater. She can do a triple Lutz. Jane is also a national champion figure-skater. She must be able to do a triple Lutz as well.

In this argument, the two objects being compared are two people who are national champion figure skaters. The characteristic being compared is the ability to do a triple Lutz. The argument claims that Jane can do a triple Lutz based on the similarity between her and Mary, who can do a triple Lutz. As with other forms of inductive arguments, there are a number of factors that must be taken into account to evaluate the strength of an argument by analogy.

Arguments from Authority

Yet another common type of inductive argument is an argument from authority. An argument from authority is an argument in which the audience is asked to accept the truth of a claim based on the fact that the claim was made by a person who is an authority about that type of claim:

> The surgeon general claims that smoking is directly linked to lung cancer. Therefore, we should accept that smoking is linked to lung cancer.

Since the Surgeon General should be knowledgeable about health issues, it would be probable that if he or she made this claim, it would be true.

The strength of arguments from authority is determined by the amount of authority the person making the claim has to be making such claims. The more authority the speaker has, the more probable the truth of the claim, and vice versa.

Deductive Argument Patterns

Just as there are typical argument patterns or forms that are always inductive, there are also argument patterns or forms that are deductive.

Categorical Arguments

The most common type of deductive argument pattern is the categorical argument. A categorical argument is one composed of categorical statements. A categorical statement, in turn, is a statement that begins with the words "all", "none" or "some." The following arguments are categorical arguments:

All dogs are mammals.
All German Shepherds are dogs.
Therefore, all German Shepherds are mammals.

All cows are mammals.
Some cows have horns.
Therefore, some mammals have horns.[5]

Arguments from definition

Arguments from definition are arguments based on the meaning of terms. A simple example is,

Bob is a bachelor

---

[5] It is important to distinguish between categorical statements and arguments which use "some," and statistical (inductive) arguments. The statements "54% of cows have horns" or "Most cows have horns" are statistical statements, while the statement "Some cows have horns" is a categorical statement. Categorical "Some" statements don't specify anything about the number or proportion of the group that have the characteristic in question, they just specify that *some* (usually understood as "at least one") of the members of the group have it. In short, statements with "some" are categorical statements (and imply that an argument is a categorical, deductive argument), and statements that specify a number or proportion are statistical statements (and imply that an argument is an inductive argument).

(All bachelors are unmarried males) – understood, not necessarily
  stated.
Therefore, Bob is an unmarried male.

Since the definition of "bachelor" is "unmarried male," if Bob is a
bachelor, he must be an unmarried male. The premise(s), then, leads to the
conclusion with certainty, so the argument is deductive.

<u>Mathematical arguments</u>

Arguments based on mathematical principles are also deductive. For
instance,

The length of the sides of this square are 5 inches.
Therefore, the area of the square is 25 in^2.

Two of the angles of this triangle measure 35° and 65°.
Therefore, the third angle of this triangle measures 80°.

1.8 – Evaluating Arguments

Once we have identified a passage as an argument and have identified
the type of argument it is, we can begin evaluating the argument. Argument
evaluation is done in two steps. The first step is to evaluate the inference (the
relationship between the premises and the conclusion). The second step is to
evaluate the truth of the premises. Although the steps are the same for both
inductive and deductive arguments, the results have different names, so we
will consider them separately.

Evaluating Inductive arguments

The first step in evaluating an argument is to evaluate the **inference**,
or the support relationship between the premises and the conclusion.
Inductive arguments are arguments in which the conclusion is only supposed
to follow with a certain degree of probability from the premises. The
evaluation of the support relationship in an inductive argument, then, is the
evaluation of the probability of the conclusion, given (assuming) the truth of
the premises.

It is of vital importance to keep track of what is being evaluated at
which step of this process. In the first step, we are evaluating the support
relationship, NOT the truth of the premises. It is easy to begin by considering
whether the premises are true or false, but this is NOT the task at this point.
The question we are considering here is best phrased as "IF the premises are

true, WOULD the conclusion be probable?" Consider the following argument:

> 97% of people who own homes in Los Angeles County irrigate their lawns.
> Bill owns a home in Los Angeles County.
> Therefore, Bill irrigates his lawn.

If we assume these premises to be true, is it probable that the conclusion would be true as well? In this case it is very probable (about 97%). We would say, then, that the support relationship is ***strong*** in this argument.

Now consider this argument:

> I know 3 people who own Jaguars (cars), and they all make over $250,000 per year.
> There's a Jaguar next to me on the freeway.
> Its owner must make over $250,000 per year.

In this case, if we assume that the premises are true, they give very weak support for the conclusion. The arguer knows only 3 people who own Jaguars, and this is a very small test group to make the generalization that someone else who owns a Jaguar would have a similar income. The support relationship in this case is very ***weak***.

Inductive arguments, after the first stage of evaluation, are said to be ***strong*** or ***weak***.

The second step of evaluation is to evaluate the **truth** of the premises. If an argument has a weak inference, this step is unnecessary. An argument must pass both tests to be a good argument, so if it has already failed the first test, there is no need to proceed to the second step. In this step, we simply ask whether ALL of the premises are true. Consider this argument,

> 85% of people have 2 heads.
> John is a person.
> Therefore, John has 2 heads.

Note that the inference in this argument is strong. IF the premises were true, it WOULD be probable (85%) that John would have 2 heads. However, it is not true that 85% of people have two heads. An argument that has any *false* premises is **UNCOGENT**, and an argument that has *all true* premises is **COGENT**.

The following chart outlines the process of evaluating inductive arguments.

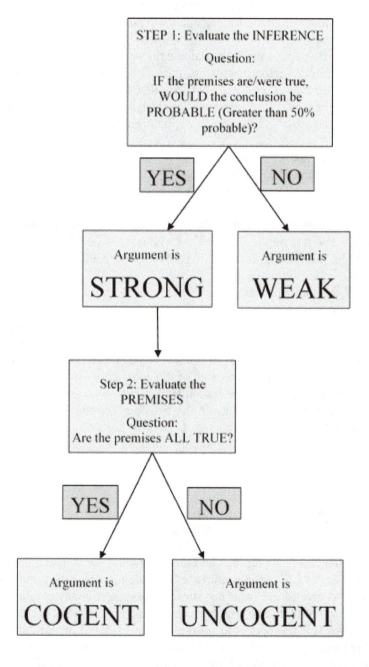

Evaluating Deductive Arguments

The steps in evaluating deductive arguments are exactly the same as the steps in evaluating inductive arguments. The results, however, have different names.

The first step, again, is to evaluate the *inference*, or support relationship. For deductive arguments, the test question is, (positively) "IF the premises are true, is it GUARANTEED that the conclusion is true as well?" or (negatively) "IF the premises are true it is POSSIBLE for the conclusion to be false?" Take the following argument:

> All dogs are mammals.
> All German Shepherds are dogs.
> Therefore, all dogs are mammals.

If these premises are true, the truth of the conclusion is guaranteed (positively), and it is impossible for the conclusion to be false (negatively). We say, then, that the argument is **VALID**. Now consider this argument:

> All dogs are mammals.
> Some mammals have hoofs.
> Therefore, some dogs have hoofs.

In this case, even if the premises are true (which they are), the truth of the premises don't guarantee the truth of the conclusion (in this case, the conclusion is in fact false). The reason is that there is no guarantee that there is any overlap between the mammals that are dogs and the mammals that have hoofs (and in fact there is no such overlap). This argument, then is **INVALID**. But some invalid arguments can have true premises AND a true conclusion. Consider:

> All dogs are mammals.
> Some mammals have canine teeth.
> Therefore, all dogs have canine teeth.

In this case, the premises and the conclusion are all true. But the argument is INVALID. It is invalid for the same reason as the previous argument was invalid. There is no guarantee that there is any overlap between the set of mammals that have canine teeth and the set of mammals that are dogs. **It is important to remember that invalid arguments can have true premises AND a true conclusion. The test of validity concerns the inference, not the truth of any statements**. Similarly, a valid argument may have all false premises and a false conclusion:

All houses are more than 1000 feet tall.
The Statue of Liberty is a house.
Therefore, the Statue of Liberty is more than 1000 feet tall.

This argument is valid, because IF the premises were true, the conclusion would be guaranteed to be true as well. The support relationship is good. However, clearly the premises are not true. This leads us to the second test, the issue of the truth of the premises.

As in inductive arguments, the truth test does not apply to invalid arguments. An argument must pass both tests to be a good argument, so if it has failed the first test, there is no need to proceed. Since the last example was valid, we do need to proceed to the second test. The premises in this example were clearly false. We say that a valid argument with some (at least one) *false* premises is **UNSOUND**. If the argument has *all true* premises (i.e., the first argument about dogs), it is both valid and **SOUND**.

The following chart outlines the process of evaluating a deductive argument.

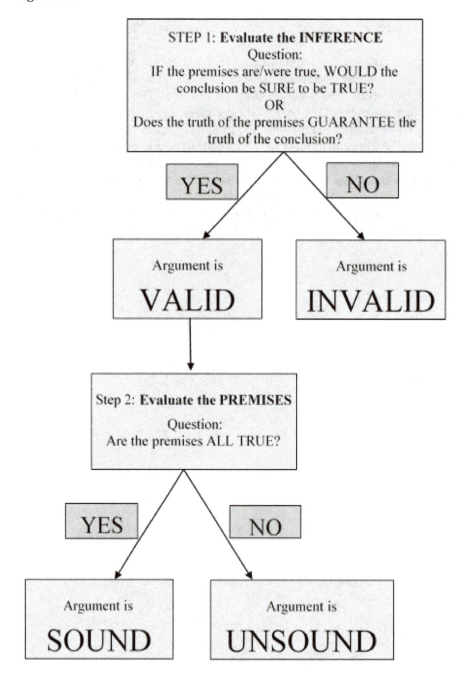

Exercises

A. State whether the following sentences are statements or not. If not, say what kind of sentence it is.
1. Robins are red.
2. Are you ready yet?
3. There is an ape-like animal living in the mountains of Washington State, that people call a Sasquatch.
4. God exists.
5. I like ice cream.
6. Go to your room!
7. Elvis Presley is still alive.
8. My team won the game!
9. Yeah!
10. I have 13 cousins.

B. State whether the following statements are fact or value statements. Then, using the criterion in the chapter, determine whether each is an objective or subjective statement.
1. Purple is the best color of eye shadow.
2. The U.S. should not have invaded Iraq.
3. California is south of Oregon.
4. The Los Angeles Lakers are the best basketball team.
5. Abortion is morally okay.
6. Geese fly south in the winter.
7. Looking at pornographic literature should be against the law.
8. There is a large animal living in Loch Ness in Scotland.
9. There are ghosts.
10. I like butterscotch pudding.

C. Evaluate the following arguments, using these criteria:
1. State whether the argument is deductive or inductive.
2. Identify the type or pattern of argument.
3. Validity/strength
   i) If the argument is deductive, determine whether it is valid or invalid.
   ii) If the argument is inductive, determine whether it is strong or weak.
4. Soundness/cogency
   i) If the argument is deductive, determine whether it is sound or unsound.
   ii) If the argument is inductive, determine whether it is cogent or uncogent.

1. My brother said that the democrats are sure to win the next election. Therefore, the democrats will win.
2. Pat is a widow. Therefore, Pat is a man.
3. I polled my friends, and 90% of them said it wasn't dangerous to drive after having a few beers. Therefore, it must not be dangerous to drive after having a few beers.
4. When a black cat crosses your path, it causes you to have particularly good luck. A black cat crossed my path this morning. So I'm expecting good luck any time.
5. All mammals have 9 hearts. All dogs are mammals. So dogs have 9 hearts.
6. Bob was just honorably discharged from the Navy Seals. He can do 100 pushups easily. Bill was also just honorably discharged from the Navy Seals. He'll be able to do 100 pushups as well.
7. A Gallup poll reported that 67% of Americans favor abolishing the death penalty. Therefore, my neighbor Sally would support abolishing the death penalty.
8. I received the correct change after giving $100 to the cashier for my $80 purchase. Therefore, I received $20 in change.
9. I left my car headlights on last night. Therefore, this morning, my car battery will be dead.
10. All fish have fins. Nemo is a fish. Therefore, Nemo has fins.

Chapter 2: Sentential Logic

2.1 – Introduction

      Symbolic Logic is a system of analyzing DEDUCTIVE arguments for validity. Although analyzing inductive arguments is an interesting and worthwhile task, and analyzing deductive arguments for soundness is also an interesting and worthwhile task, symbolic logic focuses on analyzing deductive arguments for validity. There are three branches of symbolic logic, Sentential Logic, Predicate Logic, and Modal Logic. They all employ a system of symbols to represent statements (and the arguments made of them), and a set of rules to manipulate and analyze statements and relationships between statements (especially between premises and conclusions). In this chapter we will learn Sentential Logic, then we will look at Predicate Logic in the next. We will not address Modal Logic in this textbook.

2.2 – Simple Statements

      The first step in analyzing arguments in symbolic logic is to symbolize the statements that make up the argument. The basic rule for symbolizing statements is that a simple statement will be symbolized with a single capital letter. **A *simple statement* is a statement that contains (one subject and one verb and) no operators.**[6] The following are examples of simple statements:

> Bob ran.
> Bob ran down the street.
> Bob ran down the street last Saturday at noon.

      Although these statements are of varying length and complexity, they all contain a single subject and verb ("Bob" and "ran", respectively), so they are all simple statements. Simple statements, again, are symbolized with a single capital letter. Any capital letter can stand for any simple statement, but it is helpful to choose a letter that reminds you of the statement it represents. For instance, we can symbolize any of the statements above with the capital letter, **B**.

      The following statements are not simple statements:

---

[6] Once we learn what "operator" means, we can dispense with the phrase about subject and verb.

Bob and Joe ran.
Bob ran and jumped.
Bob ran down the street and jumped into a waiting car.
Bob ran down the street, but Joe didn't go with him.

In each of these statements, there is either more than one subject (as in the first and the fourth), or more than one verb (as in the second, third, and fourth). They will each need to by symbolized by more than one statement letter. In addition to the simple statements in the statements above, there are words that connect the simple statements together ("and" in the first three, and "but" in the fourth). These words are called "connectives" or "operators." There is a limited set of such words in English (or any other language, for that matter). We will introduce symbols for these words as well. Once we have symbols for simple statements and the operators that we use to connect simple statements together, we can symbolize all English statements, no matter how complicated they are.

2.3 – Operators

An *operator* is a word or phrase that affects the truth value of a statement.

Negation

The simplest operator is the negation. A note here is important: a simple sentence must always be in the *positive* voice. That is, "Bob is not coming" is NOT a simple statement, since it is negative. A simple statement in the negative is symbolized with a sentence letter for the (positive) statement, plus a ~ ("tilde" – it's next to the number 1 on a computer keyboard. It operates in almost exactly the same way as a negative sign in math). So, "Bob is not coming" would be:

~B

Where **B** stands for "Bob is coming." It can be read as "tilde B" or "not B."

There are some other expressions that are symbolized as a negation. For instance, "It is false that Bob is coming" and "It is not the case that Bob is coming" would also be symbolized as ~B.

Conjunction

The next (and most common) operator is the conjunction. The most common conjunction is the word "and." We will use the symbol **&** to represent a conjunction. The following statements are conjunction:

> Bob ran and leaped.
> Bob and Joe ran down the street.
> Bob ran down the street, and Pete followed him.

The simple statements in the first statement above are "Bob ran" and "(Bob) leaped." We can use the letter **B** to symbolize "Bob ran" and the letter **L** to symbolize "(Bob) leaped." We would then symbolize "Bob ran and leaped" as

> B & L

Similarly, if "Bob ran down the street" is symbolized as **B** and "Joe ran down the street is symbolized as **J**, "Bob and Joe ran down the street" would be symbolized as

> B & J

Finally, if **B** symbolizes "Bob ran down the street" and **P** symbolizes "Pete followed him," "Bob ran down the street and Pete followed him" would be symbolized as

> B & P

Although "and" is the most common conjunction, it is not the only word that is symbolized with **&**. In fact, **&** is the default connector in sentential logic. It is used in every case except when one of the other connectors is specifically called for. The following connectors are always symbolized as conjunctions:

> But
> However
> Moreover
> Furthermore

Disjunction

A disjunction is an either/or statement, and is symbolized with a ∨ (wedge). The statement,

(Either) Bob will go the store or Mary will go to the store

would be symbolized,

B ∨ M

where **B** stands for "Bob will go to the store" and **M** stands for "Mary will go to the store."

Conditional

The conditional is the most difficult, but most important, operator. In its simplest form, a conditional is an "if … then" statement, such as

If Bob goes to the store, (then) Mary will go to the store.

The symbol for a conditional is → . The preceding sentence would be symbolized as

B → M

The two parts of a conditional statement have special names. The part to the left of the symbol is called the ***antecedent*** (from the Latin for "comes before"). The part to the right of the symbol is called the ***consequent*** (meaning "comes after", like "consequences"). These terms will be used throughout this text, so it is important to learn them.

There are many English expressions that express a conditional relationship. Some of them include

Implies
Entails
Is the condition for
Provided that
On the condition that

The order of the antecedent and consequent can change in everyday English for these expressions, so it is important to determine what is the condition (antecedent) for what (consequent). "A implies B" and "A entails

B" and "A is the condition for B" are all symbolized as A → B. However, if I say "Bob will go to the store *provided that* Mary goes to the store, or Bob will go to the store *on the condition* that Mary goes to the store, I am actually saying that IF Mary goes to the store, THEN Bob will (also) go to the store, which is symbolized as M → B.

Biconditional

The final operator in symbolic logic is the biconditional. A biconditional is actually a special conditional. It asserts that the conditional relationship goes both ways. For instance, "Bob will go to the store **if and only if** Mary goes to the store," I am asserting that **if** Bob goes to the store, Mary will go to the store, **and if** Mary goes to the store, Bob will go to the store. This statement can be symbolized as the conjunction of two conditionals, but a special symbol has been created for it; ≡. The statement above would be symbolized,

B ≡ M

2.4 – Symbolizing Compound Statements

Now that we understand operators, we can redefine "simple statement" without referring to few subjects and verbs A *simple statement* is **a statement that contains no operators**. A *compound statement* is **a statement that contains at least one simple statement and at least one operator**.

The simplest compound statement is a negated simple statement. It is important to remember that a negated simple statement is NOT a simple statement, but a compound statement, because it contains an operator (tilde).

The following statements are all examples of negated simple statements:

Statement	Simple Statement	Symbolization
Bob did not go to the store	B = "Bob sang"	~B
It is false that I love chocolate	C = "I love chocolate"	~C
It is not the case that Bob sings	S = "Bob sings"	~S

The rest of the operators are called ***binary*** operators. "Binary" means that they connect ***exactly two*** statements together (i.e., no more and no fewer than two). Some statements contain a number of simple statements and operators, and we must learn a process for symbolizing them so their meaning is clear. For instance, the following statement is ambiguous:

Bob bought ice cream and chocolate sauce or peanuts

It might mean "Bob bought ice cream and chocolate sauce, or Bob bought peanuts", or it might mean "Bob bought ice cream, and Bob bought chocolate sauce or peanuts." In English, we usually use commas to indicate how things are grouped. The original sentence, with commas, would be one of these two statements:

Bob bought ice cream and chocolate sauce, or peanuts.
Bob bought ice cream, and chocolate sauce or peanuts.

If we were to symbolize the original statement as

(I = "Bob bought ice cream", C = "Bob bought chocolate sauce", P = "Bob bought peanuts")

I & C ∨ P

we would encounter the same problem: we can't tell how the events (statements) are grouped. In symbolizations, we use parentheses to indicate grouping. The statement would be one of the two following statements, corresponding to the two English sentences above:

(I & C) ∨ P
I & (C ∨ P)

As we learn to analyze arguments through symbolizations, it is vital to learn to group the elements of compound statements correctly, because the order of the grouping can dramatically change the meaning of the compound statement (as it does in our example above).

There is a set of rules for grouping statements with parentheses (if you notice that these rules resemble the rules for grouping in algebra, that is no accident; they are the same rules). A statement that meets all of these rules is called a "***well-formed formula***", or a *wff*, for short.

1. A *tilde* works only on single statements.
   a. The statement may be simple or compound, but a tilde is always only attached to (the left of) a single statement.

    b. Parentheses and brackets are required to display the order of grouping for complex statements.

    c. The following statements are wffs:

~B

~(B & C)

~[(B & C) ∨ ~(D → ~F)]

~~A

    d. The following statements are not wffs:

A~

A~B

A & (B~C)

2.   The remaining operators are **binary** operators. They work according to the following rules:

    a. Parentheses are required to display the order of grouping for statements involving more than 2 statements and/or more than one binary operator.

    b. Each non-tilde operator must connect **exactly two** statements (whether simple or compound)

        i. The following statements meet this condition:

A ∨ B

(A & B) → C

[(A ≡ B) & ~(C ∨ D)] → [(B & C) → ~A]

       ii. The following statements do NOT meet this condition:

∨ B

B &

    c. If there is more than one simple statement, it must be connected to the other simple statements by **exactly** (no more and no fewer than) **one** non-tilde operator, which is placed *between* the statements.

        i. The following statements meet this condition:

A ∨ B

(A & B) → C

[(A ≡ B) & ~(C ∨ D)] → [(B & C) → ~A]

       ii. The following statements do NOT meet this condition:

AB

A & B → C

&ABC

A~B

Exercises

Translate the following statements into symbolic form. Be sure to use parentheses to indicate grouping. Use the following symbols:

"Mary sings" (M), "Bob sings" (B), "Carlita dances" (C), and "Don dances" (D)

1. Mary sings and Don dances.
2. Mary sings and Bob sings.
3. If Mary sings, then Carlita dances.
4. It is not the case that if Mary sings, then Don dances.
5. If Bob sings or Mary sings, then Carlita dances.
6. If Bob sings or Mary sings, then Don dances.
7. If Don dances or Mary sings, then Carlita dances and Bob doesn't sing.
8. If Don dances, then Carlita dances; and if Bob sings, then Mary sings.
9. If Carlita dances, then Mary sings; and Carlita dances.
10. If Mary doesn't sing, then Bob doesn't sing; and if Mary sings, then Don doesn't dance.
11. If Bob doesn't sing, then Carlita dances, and if Mary doesn't sing, then Don dances.
12. Carlita dances if and only if Bob doesn't sing.
13. Mary sings and Bob sings if and only if Carlita dances and Don dances.
14. Carlita dances, and she dances if and only if Bob sings or Don dances.
15. Carlita dances and Mary sings, if and only if Bob doesn't sing or Don doesn't dance.
16. Carlita dances and Mary sings, if and only if Bob doesn't sing; and Bob doesn't sing.
17. If either Mary or Bob sing, then Carlita dances; but Don dances if and only if Carlita dances and Bob doesn't sing.
18. If, if Carlita dances then Don dances, then Don dances if and only if Mary doesn't sing.
19. It is not the case that Mary sings and Bob sings if and only if Carlita dances and Don dances; however (and), Mary sings and Don dances if and only if Bob sings and Carlita dances.
20. If it is not the case that if Carlita dances, then Don dances, then it not the case that either Mary sings and Bob sings or that Carlita doesn't dance and Don doesn't dance.

2.5 – Truth Conditions and Truth Tables

As we learned when we learned the definition of "statement," a statement is a sentence that is EITHER true or false. This means that every statement has a *truth value*. Simply, if a statement is true, it has a truth value of "true", which we will symbolize with a capital T. Similarly, if a statement is false, it has a truth value of "false", or F.

The following statements have a truth value of T.

> Montana is a state in the United States of America.
> The sky is blue (to normal-sighted humans).
> The moon orbits the earth.
> Richard Nixon is a former president of the Unites States of America.

The following statements have a truth value of F.

> The United States borders Egypt.
> All humans have 3 heads.
> George Washington is the president of the United States of America in the year 2005 AD.
> The moon is made of green cheese.

The study of sentential logic is the study of how the truth values of compound statements are related to the truth values of the simple statements and the operators that make them up. That is, if we know the truth values of the statements that make up a compound statement, then the truth value of the compound statement is determined by the logical operator that connects them. We now turn to learning how the truth values of compound statements are related to the operators that make them up.

Characteristic Truth Table for the Negation

Suppose we have the simple statement,

All mammals have legs.

This statement is true; it has a truth value of "T". Now, suppose we *negate* that statement. To negate a statement, we add "it is false that" in front of it. We would get

It is false that all mammals have legs.

33.

The negated statement ("It is false that all mammals have hair") is false. It has a truth value of "F". Now consider,

The moon is made of green cheese.

This statement is false; it would have a truth value of "F". If we negate the statement, it becomes

It is false that the moon is made of green cheese.

The negated statement is true; it has a truth value of "T". For any statement in general, if the statement is true, its negation will be false, and if the statement is false, its negation will be true. We can symbolize this information, using our operator symbols, on a table, like this.

p	~p[7]
T	**F**
F	**T**

This table tells us that for any statement, p, its negation (~p) is false, and vice versa. Note that the truth values, T and F, go under the *tilde* on the negated statement, not under the statement. This is because *p* in the first case is true, while ~p is false, and it is *p* in the second case that is false, while it's ~p that is true. We put the truth value under the operator to indicate the truth value of the negated statement, as opposed to the truth value of the statement that's being negated.

Since this chart reveals the truth value of any negated sentence, based on the truth value of the statement that is being negated, we call it the *characteristic truth table for the negation*.

Characteristic Truth Table for the Conjunction

Suppose we have the two simple statements,

Bob sang. (B)
Mary sang. (M)

Now, suppose we connect these two statements as a conjunction:

---

[7] "p" here is a statement *variable*. It can stand for ANY statement, no matter how simple or complex, or positive or negative.

B & M

As with the negation, the truth of the conjunction ("Bob sang and Mary sang") is based on the truth values of the two statements that are conjoined. Think of a case in which Bob and Mary were at karaoke last night, and you meet someone on campus who says "Bob sang and Mary sang last night." Whether their statement is true or false depends on the facts of whether Bob sang and/or Mary sang. If it is in fact true that Bob sang and it is also true that Mary sang, then the conjunction of the two simple statements will be true. We can begin setting up a truth table for the conjunction by recording this information.

B	M	B & M
T	T	T

This simple truth table tells us that if the statement B is true and the statement M is true, the conjunction B & M is also true (note that we put the "T" under the operator, &, for the compound statement, as we put the truth value under the tilde on the truth table for the negation). But there are other possible truth values for B and M. They could each either be true or false. What if in fact, Bob sang, (B is true) but Mary didn't sing (M is false)? Then the conjunction, "Bob sang *and* Mary sang" would be false. We symbolize this on a truth table as:

B	M	B & M
T	F	F

This reads, "if B is true and M is false, then B & M is false." Similarly, if Bob didn't sing (B is false), but Mary sang (M is true), then the conjunction would also be false:

B	M	B & M
F	T	F

This line reads, "if B is false and M is true, then B & M is false." And, if Bob didn't sing (B is false) and Mary didn't sing (M is false), then the conjunction would also be false.

B	M	B & M
F	F	F

This line reads, "if B is false and M is false, then B & M is false." If we now combine all of these individual lines onto a table, replacing B and M with the variables *p* and *q,* we can construct a truth table for the &:

p	q	p & q
T	T	**T**
T	F	**F**
F	T	**F**
F	F	**F**

This table gives us all of the possible combinations of truth values for 2 statements, and the information that a conjunction is true only when BOTH the conjuncts are true, and is false in every other case.

Characteristic Truth Table for the Disjunction

All of the operators have characteristic truth tables. If we have the two statements,

Bob sang. (B)
Mary sang. (M)

We can combine them with "or" into the compound statement, "Bob sang or Mary sang," which would be symbolized by the disjunction:

B ∨ M

Remember our karaoke case: Bob and Mary were at karaoke last night and we meet someone who says "Bob sang or Mary sang." In the different situations, would this statement be true or false? The case in which Bob sang AND Mary sang (they're both true) is a special case, so we will come back to it momentarily. Let's begin with the case in which Bob sang and Mary didn't sing. In this case, the disjunction, "Bob sang OR Mary sang" would be true (since it only claims that at lease on of the two things happened. So we would get this line on our truth table:

B	M	B ∨ M
T	F	T

This line reads, "if B is true and M is false, then B ∨ M is true." If Bob sing, but Mary sang, the disjunction would still be true (since, again, at least one of the two things happened). So we would have:

B	M	B ∨ M
F	T	T

This line reads "if B is false and M is true, then B ∨ M is true."

If Bob didn't sing and Mary didn't sing, then the disjunction B ∨ M would be false:

B	M	B ∨ M
F	F	F

This line reads "if B is false and M is false, then B ∨ M is false."

Now we return to the case in which both B and M are true. In normal English, the word "or" can have one of two senses. It can have an *exclusive* sense, in which we mean that one of two things happened *but not both*. However, "or" can also mean that one or the other *or both* of two things happened. This is called the *inclusive* sense of "or." In everyday English, people most often mean the *exclusive* sense when they use "or." In sentential logic, though, we will use the *inclusive* sense. The reason for this is that we can easily symbolize the exclusive sense of "or" if we need it, so we will take the broader sense of the operator for our general sense. So, in the case in which Bob sang AND Mary sang, we will say the claim that Bob sang OR Mary sang is true. So,

B	M	B ∨ M
T	T	T

This line reads "if B is true and M is true, then B ∨ M is true."

Putting this information into the chart, replacing B and M with p and q:

p	q	p ∨ q
T	T	**T**
T	F	**T**
F	T	**T**
F	F	**F**

The thing to note about the truth table for the disjunction is that disjunctions are true on every line EXCEPT when both disjuncts are false. Knowing the general rule can be very helpful in solving sentential logic problems, so it is advisable to memorize it along with the truth table.

Characteristic Truth Table for the Conditional

A conditional statement is an "if…then…" statement. Take the two statements,

It is raining out. (R)
Bob carries his umbrella. (U)

and a conditional composed of them;

R → U
"If it is raining out (R), then Bob carries his umbrella (U)"

When we talk about truth values for conditionals, we usually talk about whether a situation *confirms* or *disconfirms* the conditional relationship. Suppose that on a particular day, it is raining (R is true), and Bob is carrying his umbrella (U is true). If someone were to say to us, "if it is raining out, then Bob carries his umbrella," with their statement be confirmed or disconfirmed by the situation? This situation would *confirm* the truth of this conditional statement, so we would say the conditional is true:

R	U	R → U
T	T	T

Now, suppose on a particular day, it is raining out (R is true), but Bob is NOT carrying his umbrella (U is false). If someone were to say "if it is raining out, then Bob carries his umbrella," the situation would disconfirm or make it false, that IF it is raining, Bob carries his umbrella (because in this case, it is raining, but he is *not* carrying his umbrella). So in this case, the conditional is false:

R	U	R → U
T	F	F

Next, suppose that on a particular day, it is not raining out (R is false), but Bob is carrying his umbrella (U is true). What if someone were to say, "if it is raining, then Bob carries his umbrella"? This situation is kind of tricky. The conditional statement does not say that Bob ONLY carries his umbrella when it is raining, it says that WHEN (IF) it is raining, he carries his umbrella. But there might be other occasions on which he carries his umbrella as well. Maybe it's hailing out today, or snowing, or there's a forecast for rain in the afternoon, or he has to get his umbrella fixed and is taking it to the umbrella store. The important thing is that this situation doesn't disconfirm the conditional – it still could be true that IF it was raining, Bob would have his umbrella. So, since this situation doesn't disconfirm the conditional, we will give it the benefit of the doubt and say it is true:

R	U	R → U
F	T	T

Finally, consider the situation in which it is NOT raining out and Bob is NOT carrying his umbrella. It's hard to know how this gives us any information about whether Bob would have his umbrella IF it was raining. But, since the situation doesn't disconfirm the conditional, we will again give it the benefit of the doubt and say it is true:

R	U	R → U
F	F	T

The characteristic truth table for the conditional, then, is:

p	q	p → q
T	T	**T**
T	F	**F**
F	T	**T**
F	F	**T**

The general rule for conditionals, from the truth table, is, a conditional is ONLY false when the antecedent (the statement on the left of the symbol) is TRUE and the consequent (the statement on the right side of the symbol) is FALSE. In every other case it is true. The conditional is the most important of the operators, for reasons that will become evident later, so it is vital to know the truth table and the general rule for conditionals.

Characteristic Truth Table for the Biconditional

Consider now the same two statements as in the previous example;

Bob carries his umbrella. (U)
It is raining out. (R)

And consider them combined into a biconditional;

U ≡ R
"Bob carries his umbrella IF AND ONLY IF it is raining out"

The meaning of a biconditional is stronger than that of a conditional. This one means that IF it is raining, Bob carries his umbrella, and IF Bob carries his umbrella, it is raining out. Now, consider the case in which Bob has his umbrella (U is true) and it is raining out (R is true). If someone were to say "Bob carries his umbrella if and only if it is raining," the situation would confirm the statement, so in this case the biconditional is true:

U	R	U ≡ R
T	T	T

Now, consider the case in which Bob has his umbrella (U is true), but it is not raining (R is false). Someone says, "Bob carries his umbrella if and only if it is raining." Unlike the conditional, the biconditional says that Bob carries his umbrella ONLY IF if it is raining; that is, he doesn't carry it when it is not raining. This case would disconfirm the biconditional, so it would be false in this case:

U	R	U ≡ R
T	F	F

Now, consider the case in which Bob doesn't have his umbrella (U is false), but it is raining out (R is true). Someone says, "Bob carries his umbrella if and only if it is raining." Since the biconditional states that he carries his umbrella IF (that is, when) it is raining, this case would disconfirm the biconditional, so it would again be false:

U	R	U ≡ R
F	T	F

Finally, in the case where Bob is not carrying his umbrella (U is false), and it is not raining (R is false), and someone says "Bob carries his umbrella if and only if it is raining." Like the case of the biconditional, we don't actually know anything for sure about the truth of the biconditional in this case, so it has not been disconfirmed, so we will again give it the benefit of the doubt and say it is true:

U	R	U ≡ R
F	F	T

The characteristic truth table for the biconditional, then, is:

p	q	p ≡ q
T	T	**T**
T	F	**F**
F	T	**F**
F	F	**T**

The general rule for the biconditional, which will help remember how to solve problems, is that the biconditional is TRUE when the statements that make it up have the SAME truth value, and FALSE when they have different truth values. A way to remember this is to think of the biconditional as an equal sign, and ask whether the two statements have equal truth values.

Summary of Characteristic Truth Tables

The combined characteristic truth tables of the binary operators are:

p	q	p & q	p ∨ q	p → q	p ≡ q
T	T	T	T	T	T
T	F	F	T	F	F
F	T	F	T	T	F
F	F	F	F	T	T

Quick rules for the different operators:
- Tildes reverse the truth value of statements they are connected to – T becomes F; F becomes T.
- Conjunctions are only true when both conjuncts are true; they are false in every other case.
- Disjunctions are only false when both disjuncts are false; they are true in every other case.
- Conditionals are only false when the antecedent (p) is true and the consequent (q) it is false; they are true in every other case.
- Biconditionals are true if both sides of the biconditional are the same, and false if both sides are different.

2.6 – Partial Truth Tables for Compound Statements

Consider the following simple statements, and their corresponding truth values:

Statement	Symbol	Truth Value
The U.S. is south of Canada	C	T
The U.S. is south of Mexico	M	F
The moon orbits the earth	O	T
The earth orbits the sun	S	T
Elvis is alive	E	F
Justin Bieber is alive	J	T

Now consider the following compound statements made up of these simple statements:

1. The U.S. is south of Canada and the U.S. is south of Mexico.
2. If the U.S. south of Canada, then it is south of Mexico.
3. The earth orbits the sun if and only if the moon orbits the earth.
4. Either Elvis is alive or Justin Bieber is alive.

These statements would have the following symbolizations:

1. C & M
2. C → M
3. S ≡ O
4. E ∨ J

We can construct a truth table to determine the truth value of any compound statement, if we know the truth values of the statements that make it up. To construct a truth table (using #1 above as an example);

1. Write the statement and put a line under it;

    <u>C & M</u>

2. Place the truth values of each simple statement below its letter;

    <u>C & M</u>
    T   F

3. Use the characteristic truth tables to determine the truth value under each operator (in this case there is only one – the &). In this case, the truth value of "C & M" is False, since that is the truth value under the & truth table when one of the conjuncts is false. The truth value of the compound statement will be the truth value placed under the operator.

C & M
T **F** F

The truth tables for the other statements, respectively, are:

2. C → M
    T **F** F

    (the second line on the truth table for the → is "F")

3. S ≡ O
    T T T

    (the first line on the truth table for the ≡ is "T")

4. E ∨ J
    F **T** T
    (the third line on the truth table for the ∨ is "T").

These examples, although compound, are still very simple. But statements in arguments can be very complex. Consider this one:

> If the U.S. is south of Canada, then it is south of Mexico, but the U.S. is south of Canada and it is not south of Mexico.

The symbolization of this statement would be:

(C → M) & (C & ~M)

This statement has several operators and parentheses. To determine its truth, we must add some rules to those above:

1. Write out the statement and put a line under it;

    (C → M) & (C & ~M)

2. Place the known truth values under each simple statement;

    $$\underline{(C \rightarrow M) \ \& \ (C \ \& \ \sim M)}$$
    T   F   T   T

3. Change the truth values for any negated simple statements;

    $$\underline{(C \rightarrow M) \ \& \ (C \ \& \ \sim M)}$$
    T   F   T   **T** F

    (Since M is false, ~M must be true)

4. Starting at the most inside parentheses, and working within parentheses first, determine the truth value for each operator.

    $$\underline{(C \rightarrow M) \ \& \ (C \ \& \ \sim M)}$$
    T **F** F   T **T** TF

    The truth value of $(C \rightarrow M)$ is F, since C is true and M is false. The truth value of $(C \ \& \ \sim M)$ is true, since C is true and ~M is true (Note: the truth value at issue here is ~M, not M).

    $$\underline{(C \rightarrow M) \ \& \ (C \ \& \ \sim M)}$$
    T **F** F **F** T **T** TF

    The truth value of the & in the middle is determined by the truth value of $(C \rightarrow M)$ (false) and of $(C \ \& \ \sim M)$ (true), since those are the two statements that are connected by the &.

5. The truth value of the statement as a whole is the LAST truth value determined, under the top-most level operator (which is called the MAIN operator). In the case above, the & in the middle is the MAIN operator, and the truth value of the overall statement is F.

Still using the statements and truth values provided, consider the truth tables for the following statements:

1. $$\underline{(C \lor M) \ \& \ (E \lor J)}$$
    T **T** F **T**   F T T

Since C is true and M is false, (C ∨ M) is true. Since E is false and J is true, (E ∨ J) is true. Since (C ∨ M) is true and (E ∨ J) is true, the & in the middle (the MAIN operator) is true, and the whole statement is true.

2. [(C → ~M) ∨ (~E ∨ J)] ≡ (O & ~S)
      T T TF   T TF T T F   T FFT

In this case, given the basic truth value assignments, (C → ~M) is true, (~E ∨ J) is true, and (O & ~S) is false. Thus, [(C → ~M) ∨ (~E ∨ J)] is a disjunction, both of whose disjuncts are true, so it is true. Thus, the whole statement is a biconditional (MAIN operator) that has a true statement on the left hand side (the disjunction) and a false statement on the right hand side (the conjunction), so it is false.

3. ~[(O ≡ S) → (~E & J)]
      F T T T T TF T T

Note that if there is a tilde outside of the outermost parentheses, it will be the MAIN operator and will reverse the truth value of everything inside the parentheses. Here, the truth value of the conditional inside the parentheses is true, but the tilde is the MAIN operator, so the final truth value for the whole sentence is false.

Exercises

Using the symbolizations from the translation exercise (repeated below), and assuming the following truth values for the simple statements, determine the truth values of each of the compound statements.

"Mary sings" (M), "Bob sings" (B), and "Carlita dances" (C) are all TRUE. "Don dances" (D) is FALSE.

1. Mary sings and Don dances.
2. Mary sings and Bob sings.
3. If Mary sings, then Carlita dances.
4. It is not the case that if Mary sings, then Don dances.
5. If Bob sings or Mary sings, then Carlita dances.

6. If Bob sings or Mary sings, then Don dances.
7. If Don dances or Mary sings, then Carlita dances and Bob doesn't sing.
8. If Don dances, then Carlita dances; and if Bob sings, then Mary sings.
9. If Carlita dances, then Mary sings; and Carlita dances.
10. If Mary doesn't sing, then Bob doesn't sing; and if Mary sings, then Don doesn't dance.
11. If Bob doesn't sing, then Carlita dances, and if Mary doesn't sing, then Don dances.
12. Carlita dances if and only if Bob doesn't sing.
13. Mary sings and Bob sings if and only if Carlita dances and Don dances.
14. Carlita dances, and she dances if and only if Bob sings or Don dances.
15. Carlita dances and Mary sings, if and only if Bob doesn't sing or Don doesn't dance.
16. Carlita dances and Mary sings, if and only if Bob doesn't sing; and Bob doesn't sing.
17. If either Mary or Bob sing, then Carlita dances; but Don dances if and only if Carlita dances and Bob doesn't sing.
18. If, if Carlita dances then Don dances, then Don dances if and only if Mary doesn't sing.
19. It is not the case that Mary sings and Bob sings if and only if Carlita dances and Don dances; however (and), Mary sings and Don dances if and only if Bob sings and Carlita dances.
20. If it is not the case that if Carlita dances, then Don dances, then it not the case that either Mary sings and Bob sings or that Carlita doesn't dance and Don doesn't dance.

2.7 – *Complete Truth Tables*

In the previous examples, we knew the truth values for the simple statements that made up the compound statements. However, logicians often want to consider the possible truth values for statement forms when the values of the simple statements are not known. In order to do this, logicians use a *complete truth table* for a statement or set of statements. Consider the statement:

(A & B) ∨ (A ∨ B)

We don't know the truth values for A and B (we don't even know what statements they stand for!). But we can determine, for *any* combination of truth values for A and B, what the truth value of this compound statement would be.

Constructing a Complete Truth Table

To construct a complete truth table, we have to consider all of the possible combinations of truth values for the simple statements in the table. Since each statement can have 2 truth values (T or F), there is a formula that will reveal how many possible combinations there are. One statement has 2 truth values (T or F). With two statements, say, A and B, each of the statements can be either true or false. So, A can be true and B true, or A can be true, and B false, or A can be false, and B true, or A can be false, and B false. That is, for each possible value for A (T or F), B can have either value (T or F). So, we have to multiply the possibilities for A by the possibilities for B, or 2 X 2, which gives us 4 possible combinations. If you recall the characteristic truth tables, which were truth tables for two letters, each has 4 lines, or combinations. We draw a table with these possible values like this:

A	B
T	T
T	F
F	T
F	F

Note that on this table, under the A, we put two Ts followed by two Fs and under the B we put one T followed by one F, alternating. We will refer back to this pattern as our statements become more complex.

Once we have laid out the truth value combinations for the simple statements, we put the statement whose truth table we want to investigate on the line next to the simple statements. The truth table for the statement above will look like this:

A	B	(A & B) ∨ (A ∨ B)
T	T	
T	F	
F	T	
F	F	

Now, working across, we can enter the truth values for A and B and work out the truth value of the compound statement for that set of truth values:

A	B	(A & B) ∨ (A ∨ B)
T	T	T T T T T T T
T	F	
F	T	
F	F	

A	B	(A & B) ∨ (A ∨ B)
T	T	T T T T T T T
T	F	T F F T T T F
F	T	
F	F	

A	B	(A & B) ∨ (A ∨ B)
T	T	T T T T T T T
T	F	T F F T T T F
F	T	F F F T F T T
F	F	

A	B	(A & B) ∨ (A ∨ B)
T	T	T T T T T T T
T	F	T F F T T T F
F	T	F F F T F T T
F	F	F F F F F F F

49.

Once the truth table is completed, the set of truth values under the main operator (represented below by the box) is said to be the *truth table* for this statement.

A	B	(A & B) ∨ (A ∨ B)
T	T	T T T **T** T T T
T	F	T F F **T** T T F
F	T	F F F **T** F T T
F	F	F F F **F** F F F

This particular statement is true in every case except when A and B are both false. There is nothing particularly interesting about this example, but other cases have interesting patterns.

Suppose we have this statement:

(A → B) & (A → ~C)

Now we have three simple statements. How many possible combinations of truth values are there? There are two possibilities for A (T or F), two for B (T or F), and two for C (T or F). We have to multiply the possibilities: 2 X 2 X 2 = 8. There are 8 possible truth value combinations for 3 statements.

The relationship between the number of letters and the number of truth value combinations for truth tables is 2^n, where n is the number of simple statements. That means that every additional statement doubles the number of possible combinations, or the number of rows on the truth table. You can see that truth tables will become very large and unwieldy very quickly. This is one of their main limitations.

To complete the truth table for our current example, with 3 simple statements (A, B, and C), we begin by filling out the combinations for these statements. The standard (and most efficient) procedure is to begin with the right-most letter (C) and place alternating Ts and Fs under it, for however many rows are required (in this case, 8):

A	B	C
		T
		F
		T
		F
		T
		F
		T
		F

Next, move to the next letter to the left, and double the number of Ts and Fs that are repeated. In this case, we will put 2 Ts followed by 2 Fs, alternating, under the B.

A	B	C
	T	T
	T	F
	F	T
	F	F
	T	T
	T	F
	F	T
	F	F

Next, move to the next letter to the left, and again double the number of Ts and Fs that are repeated. In this case, we will put 4 Ts followed by 4 Fs, alternating, under the A.

A	B	C
T	T	T
T	T	F
T	F	T
T	F	F
F	T	T
F	T	F
F	F	T
F	F	F

This procedure can be repeated for any number of simple letters. That is, if there were a 4th letter, there would be 16 rows, and the left-most letter would have 8 Ts followed by 8 Fs, etc.

Now that the truth value combinations are completed, we can determine the truth value of the statement for each row, using the method we have learned. That is, place the Ts and Fs under the simple statements on each row, and compute the truth value of the complete statement on each row.

The *truth table for a statement*, when a complete truth table has been completed, is the set of Ts and Fs in the *column under the main operator* (here identified with a box).

A	B	C	(A → B) & (A → ~C)
T	T	T	T T T **F** T **F** F T
T	T	F	T T T **T** T T TF
T	F	T	T **F** T **F** T **F** F T
T	F	F	T **F** F **F** T T TF
F	T	T	F T T **T** F T TF
F	T	F	F T T **T** F T F T
F	F	T	F T F **T** F T F T
F	F	F	F T F **T** F T TF

Again, this is not too interesting. We will now move to look at some more interesting patterns for statements.

2.8 – Truth Table Patterns for Statements

Truth Table Patterns for Single Statements

Tautologies or Logical Truths

Note the following truth table:

A	B	A ∨ (B ∨ ~B)
T	T	T **T** T T FT
T	F	T **T** F T T F
F	T	F **T** T T FT
F	F	F **T** F T T F

The statement is true under every truth value assignment (every row on the truth table). Any statement that has this pattern is called a *tautology* or a *logical truth*.

Logical Contradiction or Logical Falsehood

Now, note this truth table:

A	B	A & (B & ~B)
T	T	T **F** T F FT
T	F	T **F** F F TF
F	T	F **F** T F FT
F	F	F **F** F F TF

The statement is false on every truth value assignment. Any statement that has this pattern is said to be *logically contradictory* or a *logical falsehood*.

Contingent Statements

A statement that is neither logically true nor logically false (that is, it has both Ts and Fs on its truth table) is said to be *contingent*.

Truth Table Patterns for Pairs of Statements

Truth tables may also be used to compare pairs of statements to each other. There are several relationships between pairs of statements that are of interest to logicians.

Logically Equivalent Statements

Consider the following statements:

A → B   ~A ∨ B

To construct a truth table for a pair of statements, we follow the same procedure as before, but we put both statements on the table, next to each other:

A	B	A → B	~A ∨ B
T	T	T **T** T	FT **T** T
T	F	T **F** F	FT **F** F
F	T	F **T** T	TF **T** T
F	F	F **T** F	TF **T** F

The truth tables for these two statements are exactly the same. Where the one is true, the other is true and where the one is false, the other is false. Two statements that have exactly the same truth table are said to be *logically equivalent*.

Logically Contradictory Statements

Now consider these statements:

$A \rightarrow B$ $A \,\&\, {\sim}B$

Their truth table would be:

A	B	A → B	A & ~B
T	T	T **T** T	T **F** FT
T	F	T **F** F	T **T** TF
F	T	F **T** T	F **F** FT
F	F	F **T** F	F **F** TF

The truth tables for these two statements are exactly *opposite*. Where the one is true, the other is false and where the one is false, the other is true. Two statements that have exactly the opposite truth tables are said to be *logically contradictory*.

If two statements have the same truth values on some rows and different truth values on other rows, they are simply neither logically equivalent nor logically contradictory.

Exercises

Full Truth Tables for single statements

Use a full truth table to evaluate the following statements. Determine whether each statement is a tautology, a contradiction, or contingent.

1. (A & B) & (A & ~B)
2. (A → B) → (A & ~B)
3. (A ∨ B) ∨ (~A ∨ ~B)
4. ((A → B) ∨ C) & ~C
5. (M & D) ≡ (~B → ~D)

Full Truth Tables for pairs of statements

Use a full truth table to evaluate the following statements. Determine whether
each pair is logically equivalent, logically contradictory, or neither.

1. A → B   ~A ∨ B
2. ~(A ∨ B)   ~A & ~B
3. ~(A & B)   ~A ∨ ~B
4. A → (B → C)   (A → B) → C
5. A → (B → C)   (A & B) → C

2.9 – Truth Table Patterns for Sets of Statements

In addition to being interested in truth table patterns for single statements and pairs of statements, logicians are interested in truth tables for *sets* of statements. This interest is directly related to the analysis of the validity of arguments, because, if you remember, an argument *is* a *set* of statements. That means we can use truth tables to analyze arguments for validity, which is our overall objective.

Consistency

There is one pattern for sets of statements that we will discuss before looking at truth tables for arguments, though. Consider the set of statements comprised of two statements related by each of the operators:

P	Q	P & Q	P ∨ Q	P → Q	P ≡ Q
T	T	T T T	T T T	T T T	T T T
T	F	T F F	T T F	T F F	T F T
F	T	F F T	F T T	F T T	F F T
F	F	F F F	F T F	F T F	F T F

One of the questions logicians ask about sets of sentences is whether it is possible for them *all to be true at the same time*. In terms of truth tables, this question is the question of whether there are any *rows* on the truth table on which all of the statements are true (since each row on the truth table represents one unique combination of truth values under which all of the statements are being considered). In the example above, there is such a row, the first row. Each of the statements is true on this row of the truth table.

P	Q	P & Q	P ∨ Q	P → Q	P ≡ Q
T	T	T T T	T T T	T T T	T T T

A set of statements is *consistent* if and only if there is at least one row on their truth table on which they are *all* true. Note that only one row is needed to show consistency. It makes no difference how many rows there on which the statements are all true, or how many rows there are on which they are *not* all true, or even if there are rows on which they are all *false*. The only issue here is whether there is *one* row on which they are all *true*. The issue of consistency will become very important in later discussions.

Validity

The next (and final) issue for truth tables is the issue of validity. Recalling our definition of validity, an argument is valid if and only if it is impossible for the conclusion to be false WHILE the premises are true. This means that **an argument is valid if and only if there is NO row on the truth table in which the premises are true and the conclusion is false**. If we construct a truth table for an argument, and there is a single case (a single row) on the truth table on which the *conclusion is false* while the *premises are all true*, the argument is invalid. Only if there it is NO such case is the argument valid. Consider the following argument:

A & B
A → B
∴ A & ~B

The truth table for this argument would be constructed like the truth table for a set of statements:

A	B	A & B	A → B	∴ A ∨ ~B
T	T	T **T** T	T **T** T	T **T** F T
T	F	T **F** F	T **F** F	T **T** T F
F	T	F **F** T	F **T** T	F **F** F T
F	F	F **F** F	F **T** F	F **F** T F

The question regarding this truth table is, again, whether there are *any rows on which the premises are true and the conclusion is false*. In this case, the answer is "no." On the first row, the premises AND the conclusion are true. On the second row, both premises are false while the conclusion is true. On the third and fourth rows, although the conclusion is false, the first premise is false. So there are NO rows on which the premises are ALL true while the conclusion is false. So this argument is VALID.

Now consider this argument:

A & (B ∨ C)
(A ∨ B) → C
∴ A → (B & ~C)

Since this argument has 3 terms, the truth table will have 8 rows; we will fill them out as we did for single statements, except we have to put truth values under each letter in each statement:

A	B	C	A & (B ∨ C)	(A ∨ B) → C	∴ A → (B & C)
T	T	T	T T T T T	T T T T T	T T T T T
T	T	F	T T T T F	T T T F T	T F T F F
T	F	T	T T F T T	T T T T T	T F T F F
T	F	F	T F F F F	T T F F F	T F T F F
F	T	T	F F T T T	F T T T T	F T T T T
F	T	F	F F T T F	F T T F F	F T T F F
F	F	T	F F F T F	F F F T T	F T F F T
F	F	F	F F F F F	F F F T F	F T F F F

The question is, *are there any rows on this truth table in which the premises are ALL true and the conclusion is false?* There is such a row; the third row, which looks like this:

A	B	C	A & (B ∨ C)	(A ∨ B) → C	∴ A → (B & C)
T	F	T	T ⓉF T T	T T T ⓉT	T ⒻT F F

On this row, when A is true, B is false, and C is true, both of the premises are true, and the conclusion is false. This shows that there is a case in which the premises are true and the conclusion is false, and this shows the argument to be INVALID. Remember, if there is ONE such row, that is all that is needed to show that an argument is invalid. In order for an argument to be valid, there must be NO rows on the truth table on which the premises are all true while the conclusion is false.

Exercises

Truth tables for consistency

Use a full truth table to test each of the following sets of statements for consistency. Be able to explain what indicates that the statements are consistent or inconsistent.

1. A & ~B   A ∨ B   A → ~B
2. A ≡ (A ∨ B)   (A & ~B) ≡ (A & B)   A & B
3. A ∨ (A ∨ B)   A & (A & ~B)   A → B
4. A ∨ (B → C)   (A & B) → ~C   B & ~C
5. B ≡ (C & D)   ~B & (C & D)   B ∨ (C ∨ D)

Truth tables for validity

Use a full truth table to test each of the following arguments for validity. Be able to explain what indicates that the argument is valid or invalid. ∴ signals the conclusion.

1. A & ~B   A ∨ B   ∴ A → ~B
2. A ≡ (A ∨ B)   (A & ~B) ≡ (A & B)   ∴ A & B
3. A ∨ (A ∨ B)   A & (A & ~B)   ∴ A → B
4. A ∨ (B → C)   (A & B) → ~C   ∴ B & ~C
5. B ≡ (C & D)   ~B & (C & D)   ∴ B ∨ (C ∨ D)

2.10 – Shortened Truth Tables for Validity and Consistency

Since every added simple statement doubles the number of lines on a truth table, truth tables can become very large and unwieldy very quickly. In this section we will learn some methods for shortening the truth table method of analysis. Note, however, that with shortcuts come increased chances of making errors. The full truth table method, although it can be time-consuming, will always yield a correct answer with little chance of making mistakes.

The first shortcut method is a shortcut for filling out truth tables, even if a full truth table is to be constructed. For it, rather than making the columns of Ts and Fs on the left side of the table, and then transferring them over to the statements, it is quicker just to put the columns of Ts and Fs directly under the statements. The critical issue with this method is that *every* time a letter shows up in *any* statement it must get the *same* pattern of Ts and Fs under it, or else the truth table becomes invalid. For example:

A & (B ∨ C)			(A ∨ B) → C			A → (B & C)		
T	T	T	T	T	T	T	T	T
T	T	F	T	T	F	T	T	F
T	F	T	T	F	T	T	F	T
T	F	F	T	F	F	T	F	F
F	T	T	F	T	T	F	T	T
F	T	F	F	T	F	F	T	F
F	T	F	F	T	F	F	T	F
F	F	F	F	F	F	F	F	F

Now, we have all of the truth value combinations under the letters, and we have written considerably fewer Ts and Fs! Note carefully that EVERY A in the statements has 4 Ts followed by 4 Fs, EVERY B has two Ts followed by 2 Fs, alternating, and EVERY C has one T followed by one F, alternating. Again, EVERY letter has to have exactly the same column EACH time it shows up in any statement, and wherever it shows up in the statement, whether it is the first or last letter, or somewhere in between.

Consistency

The shortcut method can be used to test sets of statements for consistency. Taking the following set of statements, we begin by assigning truth values directly under the letters (in the interest of time, any negated statement will be immediately changed):

A ∨ (B ∨ C)			(~A & ~B) → C			(B ≡ C) & ~A		
T	T	T	FT	FT	T	T	F	FT
T	T	F	FT	FT	F	T	T	FT
T	F	T	FT	TF	T	F	T	FT
T	F	F	FT	TF	F	F	F	FT
F	T	T	TF	FT	T	T	T	TF
F	T	F	TF	FT	F	T	F	TF
F	F	T	TF	TF	T	F	T	TF
F	F	F	TF	TF	F	F	F	TF

When we are examining truth tables for consistency, we are looking for any row on which ALL of the statements are TRUE. So **any row in which any of the statements are false can be abandoned**. One strategy is to just go down one of the columns (usually doing simpler statements first is quicker – like conjunctions, which are only be true in one case). Another is to look for patterns in which statements will turn out to be false. This is where good knowledge of the basic truth tables is very valuable; it will help you see quickly when statements will be false. For instance, the conjunction on the far right will be false whenever ~A (the right conjunct) is false (whatever (B ≡ C) is), and ~A is false on the first 4 rows. I will place an "X" under the main operator of that statement in those those rows to show that we have abandoned that row – it can't be the rower looking for.

A ∨ (B ∨ C)			(~A & ~B) → C			(B ≡ C) & ~A		
T	T	T	FT	FT	T	T	T X	FT
T	T	F	FT	FT	F	T	F X	FT
T	F	T	FT	TF	T	F	T X	FT
T	F	F	FT	TF	F	F	F X	FT
F	T	T	TF	FT	T	T	T	TF
F	T	F	TF	FT	F	T	F	TF
F	F	T	TF	TF	T	F	T	TF
F	F	F	TF	TF	F	F	F	TF

Similarly, if the left conjunct of a conjunction is false, the conjunction will be false, so whenever (B ≡ C) is false, the third statement will also be false:

A ∨ (B ∨ C)			(~A & ~B) → C			(B ≡ C) & ~A			
T	T	T	FT	FT	T	T	T	✗	FT
T	T	F	FT	FT	F	T	F	✗	FT
T	F	T	FT	TF	T	F	T	✗	FT
T	F	F	FT	TF	F	F	F	✗	FT
F	T	T	TF	FT	T	T	T		TF
F	T	F	TF	FT	F	T F F	✗	TF
F	F	T	TF	TF	T	F F T	✗	TF
F	F	F	TF	TF	F	F	F		TF

We have now eliminated 6 of the 8 rows without even looking at the first two statements! Regarding the first statement, it is a disjunction within a disjunction, so it will be false if all of the simple statements are false, which they are on row 8:

A ∨ (B ∨ C)				(~A & ~B) → C			(B ≡ C) & ~A			
T		T	T	FT	FT	T	T	T ✗	FT
T		T	F	FT	FT	F	T	F ✗	FT
T		F	T	FT	TF	T	F	T ✗	FT
T		F	F	FT	TF	F	F	F ✗	FT
F		T	T	TF	FT	T	T	T	TF
F		T	F	TF	FT	F	T F F ✗	TF
F		F	T	TF	TF	T	F F T ✗	TF
F	✗	F	F F	TF	TF	F	F	F	TF

Now, the only row we have left to examine more closely is row 5. Working out the truth values there, we get:

A ∨ (B ∨ C)				(~A & ~B) → C				(B ≡ C) & ~A			
T		T	T	FT	FT		T	T T	✗	FT
T		T	F	FT	FT		F	T F	✗	FT
T		F	T	FT	TF		T	F T	✗	FT
T		F	F	FT	TF		F	F F	✗	FT
F ⓣ	T	T T	TF F FT ⓣ		T	T T T ⓣ	TF
F		T	F	TF	FT		F	T F F	✗	TF
F		F	T	TF	TF		T	F F T	✗	TF
F ✗	F	F F	TF	TF		F	F F		TF

On this row, all of the statements come out to be true. So the set of statements is consistent (remember, one row on which all of the statements are true is all that is necessary to show consistency).

The procedure for the shortcut method of testing for consistency are:

1. Fill out the columns of truth values under each of the simple statements in the set.
2. Begin completing the truth values for the compound statements. Begin with the simplest statement or a statement that will quickly yield Fs.
3. **Eliminate** any row on which *any statement is FALSE* (place an X on the F under the main operator of the false statement in these rows, or draw a line through the entire row).
4. As soon as you have a single row on which all the statements are TRUE, you can declare the statements **CONSISTENT**.
5. If, after examining ALL rows, you have NO rows on which all the statements are TRUE, you can declare the statements **INCONSISTENT**.

Validity

When we evaluate an argument for validity, we are looking for *a row in which the premises are all TRUE and the conclusion is FALSE*. That means that any row on which the conclusion is TRUE is *not* a row that can show the argument to be invalid. So it is quicker to start by determining the truth value of the conclusion on each row before even looking at the premises. If we do that, we get this result in this example:

A & (B ∨ C)			(A ∨ B) → C			∴ A → (B & C)				
T	T	T	T	T	T	T	**T**	T	T	T
T	T	F	T	T	F	T	**F**	T	F	F
T	F	T	T	F	T	T	**F**	F	F	T
T	F	F	T	F	F	T	**F**	F	F	F
F	T	T	F	T	T	F	**T**	T	T	T
F	T	F	F	T	F	F	**T**	T	F	F
F	F	T	F	F	T	F	**T**	F	F	T
F	F	F	F	F	F	F	**T**	F	F	F

Now we can look at the truth table for the conclusion and rule out all rows on which the conclusion is NOT false (true). That eliminates all but three of the rows, because the conclusion is true on all but three of the rows (it is true on rows 1, 5, 6, 7, and 8, and it is false on rows 2,3, and 4). We can put an X through the T on all of the rows on which the conclusion is true, which signals that we don't have to look at those rows any more (or you can cross out the entire row). It is also helpful to circle the Fs, showing that these are rows we have to pay attention to.

A & (B ∨ C)			(A ∨ B) → C			∴ A → (B & C)				
T	T	T	T	T	T	T	⊠	T	T	T
T	T	F	T	T	F	T	Ⓕ	T	F	F
T	F	T	T	F	T	T	Ⓕ	F	F	T
T	F	F	T	F	F	T	Ⓕ	F	F	F
F	T	T	F	T	T	F	⊠	T	T	T
F	T	F	F	T	F	F	⊠	T	F	F
F	F	T	F	F	T	F	⊠	F	F	T
F	F	F	F	F	F	F	⊠	F	F	F

Now, we only have to work out the truth values of the *premises* on three rows (since they are the only ones that can show the argument to be invalid, since the conclusion is false on them). So we've already shortened our work considerably.

When we look at the premises on these three rows we can think this: if we come across a premise that is false, we can eliminate that row, because if there is a false premise, it can't be a row on which the premises are all true and the conclusion is false.

On rows 2 and 4, the second premise is false. So we can place an X through the F and abandon those rows.

A & (B ∨ C)			(A ∨ B) → C			∴ A → (B & C)				
T	T	T	T	T	T	T	⊠	T	T	T
T	T	F	T T T ⊠ F			T	Ⓕ	T	F	F
T	F	T	T	F	T	T	Ⓕ	F	F	T
T	F	F	T T F ⊠ F			T	Ⓕ	F	F	F
F	T	T	F	T	T	F	⊠	T	T	T
F	T	F	F	T	F	F	⊠	T	F	F
F	F	T	F	F	T	F	⊠	F	F	T
F	F	F	F	F	F	F	⊠	F	F	F

The only row left to check now is row 3. All of the premises come out to be true on this row, so (as we saw before) the argument is invalid. But we determined this with much less work than before.

Sentential Logic

A & (B ∨ C)	(A ∨ B) → C	∴ A → (B & C)
T T T	T T T	T ⊠ T T T
T T F	T T T ⊠ F	T Ⓕ T F F
T Ⓣ F T T	T T F Ⓣ T	T Ⓕ F F T
T F F	T T F ⊠ F	T Ⓕ F F F
F T T	F T T	F ⊠ T T T
F T F	F T F	F ⊠ T F F
F F T	F F T	F ⊠ F F T
F F F	F F F	F ⊠ F F F

The general rules for this shortcut for validity are:

1. Begin filling out the columns of T's and F's under the simple statements. Then begin to determine the truth values of the conclusion.
2. **Eliminate** any row on which the *conclusion is TRUE* (place an X on the T under the main operator of the conclusion in these rows, or cross out the entire row).
3. For the rows on which the conclusion is FALSE, begin determining the truth values of the premises.
4. **Eliminate** any row on which any *premise is FALSE* (place an X on the F under the main operator of the false premise in these rows, or draw a line through the entire row).
5. As soon as you have a single row on which the premises are TRUE and the conclusion is FALSE, you can declare the argument **INVALID**.
6. If, after examining ALL rows, there are NO rows on which the premises are TRUE and the conclusion is FALSE you can declare the argument **VALID**.

Exercises

Shortened truth tables for consistency

Use a shortened truth table to test each of the following sets of statements for consistency. Be able to explain what indicates that the statements are consistent or inconsistent.

1. A ∨ (B → C)   (A & B) → ~C   B & ~C
2. B ≡ (C & D)   ~B & (C → D)   B ∨ (C ∨ D)
3. A & (B & ~C)   B ∨ (~A ∨ ~C)   (C ≡ A) & ~B

65.

4. (B & A) ≡ (A → ~C)   (A ∨ B) → C   (B & C) → (A & B)
5. (A ∨ B) ≡ (B → ~C)   ((A & B) → ~C) ≡ B   (A & B) & ~C

Shortened truth tables for validity

Use a shortened truth table to test each of the following arguments for validity. Be able to explain what indicates that the arguments are consistent or inconsistent.

1. A ∨ (B → C)   (A & B) → ~C   ∴ B & ~C
2. B ≡ (C & D)   ~B & (C → D)   ∴ B ∨ (C ∨ D)
3. A & (B & ~C)   B ∨ (~A ∨ ~C)   ∴ (C ≡ A) & ~B
4. (B & A) ≡ (A → ~C)   (A ∨ B) → C   ∴ (B & C) → (A & B)
5. (A ∨ B) ≡ (B → ~C)   ((A & B) → ~C) ≡ B   ∴ (A & B) & ~C

Sentential Logic

2.11 – The Indirect Method

Consistency

The shortcut methods we have just learned will shorten the process of constructing truth tables considerably. But they are still limited. What if you have an argument that has 5 simple statements? The truth table will have $2^5 = 32$ lines! Even the shortcut method will be cumbersome and slow for that. But there is an even shorter method.

Knowing the characteristic truth tables of the operators (it is vital that you know them by heart by this time), it is possible to limit the number of rows that have to be considered to only a few, even when the number of simple statements is large. Consider the following set of statements, and the question of consistency:

A & B   A → C   B → D   (C & D) → ~A

There are 4 simple statements in this set, so it would require a truth table of 34 lines, which is very impractical. However, we know what we are looking for. We are looking for a row on which all of the statements are true. We can try to *construct* such a row for these statements. If we are able to, we will know that the set is consistent; if not, we will know it is not consistent. To begin constructing a test-row, we place a T in a circle under each of the main operators of the set of statements, symbolizing what we want to show:

A & B   A → C   B → D   (C & D) → ~A
 Ⓣ   Ⓣ   Ⓣ   Ⓣ

Next, we consider the main operators of each of the statements. They are, from left to right; & and 3 →. Now we think about the characteristic truth tables of these operators. We ask, are there any operators that can be true in only a limited number of cases? The → is true in 3 of four rows of its truth table, but the & is only true on one of its four rows (the case in which the left and right conjuncts are both true). So, we know that the first statement, in order to be true, must be true on both sides of the operator - if either a or B are false, A & B will be false. So, if this set is consistent, A and B must both be true. We place a T under each of those simple statements.

A & B   A → C   B → D   (C & D) → ~A
TⓉT   Ⓣ   Ⓣ   Ⓣ

67.

A simple statement in a set of statements must always have the same truth value. So we can place a T under each A and B anywhere in the set.

A & B	A → C	B → D	(C & D) → ~A
T(T)T	T(T)	T(T)	(T) FT

Note: since the A in the last statement is negated, ~A must be false.

The process now becomes one of filling in truth values in trying to complete all the statements. Remember, we are *trying* to make all the statements true. You must attempt to supply truth values that will make the statements true.

A & B	A → C	B → D	(C & D) → ~A
T(T)T	T(T) T	T(T)	(T) FT

Next, we look at A → C. A must be true. We want the conditional to be true. If C were false, the conditional would be false – so C can't be false; it must be true.

A & B	A → C	B → D	(C & D) → ~A
T(T)T	T(T) T	T(T)T	(T) FT

Next, we look at B → D. B must be true. We want the conditional to be true. If D were false, the conditional would be false – so D can't be false; it must be true.

A & B	A → C	B → D	(C & D) → ~A
T(T)T	T(T) T	T(T)T	(T) FT

Now we look at the last statement. We know that A is true and ~A is false. We also know that C is true and D is true; we can place those truth values under the letters.

A & B	A → C	B → D	(C & D) → ~A
T(T)T	T(T) T	T(T)T	T T (X) FT

Now we run into a problem. If C and D are both true, then C & D is true. But if the conditional has true on the left and false on the right, like this one would, it is false! If we try to fix this by making either C or D false, it would make the 2nd or 3rd statement false. So it turns out that there is no way to make all of the statements true at the same time. I will indicate this by placing an "X" over the main operator of the statement that fails (it could

68.

always be one of several statements in any set). That means the set is **inconsistent**. And we only had to look at one row on the truth table to determine that. Let's go through another example:

(A & B) & C   (D ∨ E) → ~B   (E & A) ≡ G   F ∨ D

      There are 6 simple statements in this set, so it would require a truth table of 64 lines, which is very impractical. However, we know what we are looking for. We are looking for a row on which all of the statements are true. We can try to *construct* such a row for these statements. We place a T in a circle under each of the main operators:

(A & B) & C   (D ∨ E) → ~B   (E & A) ≡ G   F ∨ D
     Ⓣ   Ⓣ   Ⓣ   Ⓣ

      Next, we consider the main operators of each of the statements. They are, from left to right; &, → , ≡, and ∨. The → is true in 3 of four rows of its truth table; the ≡ is true on two of four rows, the ∨ is true on 3 of four rows, but the & is only true on one of its four rows. We know that the first statement, in order to be true, must be true on both sides of the operator. That is, A & B (the compound statement) must be true, and C must be true. We can fill these truth values in under the operators:

(A & B) & C   (D ∨ E) → ~B   (E & A) ≡ G   F ∨ D
  T   Ⓣ T   Ⓣ   Ⓣ   Ⓣ

      Now, A & B is another conjunction. That means that, again, both of its conjuncts, A and B, must be true in order for it to be true. So the first statement, if true, must look like this:

(A & B) & C   (D ∨ E) → ~B   (E & A) ≡ G   F ∨ D
  T T T Ⓣ T   Ⓣ   Ⓣ   Ⓣ

      We can now take this information and use it to determine the truth values of other statements, because a simple statement must have the same truth value wherever it shows up on a particular row of a truth table. Moving on to the second statement, since we already know that B must be true, ~B must be false:

(A & B) & C	(D ∨ E) → ~B	(E & A) ≡ G	F ∨ D
T T T ⓉT	ⓉFT	Ⓣ	Ⓣ

A conditional statement with a false consequent will only be true if it also has a false antecedent (because T → F = F , but F → F = T). So (D ∨ E) must be false for the conditional to come out true. But D and E must both be false for (D ∨ E) to be false. So we can complete the truth values for the second statement:

(A & B) & C	(D ∨ E) → ~B	(E & A) ≡ G	F ∨ D
T T T ⓉT	F F F ⓉFT	Ⓣ	Ⓣ

We now have two true statements, and more information. We know that E is false and A is true, so (E & A) In the third statement will be false:

(A & B) & C	(D ∨ E) → ~B	(E & A) ≡ G	F ∨ D
T T T ⓉT	F F F ⓉFT	F F T Ⓣ	Ⓣ

If (E & A) is false, the biconditional will be only true if G is false (remember we *want* to make it true):

(A & B) & C	(D ∨ E) → ~B	(E & A) ≡ G	F ∨ D
T T T ⓉT	F F F ⓉFT	F F T ⓉF	Ⓣ

The last statement is a disjunction, and we know that D is false. We want to make the statement true if we can. Is there a truth value that we can assign to F that will make the disjunction true? Yes; a disjunction is true if EITHER of its disjuncts are true. If we make F true, it will make the disjunction true.

(A & B) & C	(D ∨ E) → ~B	(E & A) ≡ G	F ∨ D
T T T ⓉT	F F F ⓉFT	F F T ⓉF	TⓉF

Now consider what we have done. We have discovered a set of truth values that will make ALL of the statements true. We can now answer the question, is it possible for all of these statements to be true at the same time? The answer is "yes," even though we have considered only one row. But, remember, for consistency, *one* row on which all of the statements are true at the same time is all we need.

Use the same operation to test this set.

(A & B) & ~C   (D ∨ E) → ~B   (E ∨ F) ≡ C   F ∨ C

We begin the test in the same way, by putting Ts under all the main operators, then making the first statement true. In this case, it is ~C that must be made true. This means that C must be false:

(A & B) & ~C   (D ∨ E) → ~B   (E ∨ F) ≡ C   F ∨ C
 T T T (T) TF   (T)   (T)   (T)

We take the information from the first statement and make the second statement true:

(A & B) & ~C   (D ∨ E) → ~B   (E ∨ F) ≡ C   F ∨ C
 T T T (T) TF   F F F (T) FT   (T)   (T)

We know C is false (from statement 1), so we can put it into the last statement (the order of completing the statements makes no difference):

(A & B) & ~C   (D ∨ E) → ~B   (E ∨ F) ≡ C   F ∨ C
 T T T (T) TF   F F F (T) FT   (T)   (T) F

To make that statement true, now, we have to make F true:

(A & B) & ~C   (D ∨ E) → ~B   (E ∨ F) ≡ C   F ∨ C
 T T T (T) TF   F F F (T) FT   (T)   T (T) F

The F in the third statement is true, and the E in the third statement is false (from the second statement), which makes the disjunction (E ∨ F) true:

(A & B) & ~C   (D ∨ E) → ~B   (E ∨ F) ≡ C   F ∨ C
 T T T (T) TF   F F F (T) FT   F T T (T)   T (T) F

But now we have a problem. We already know that C has to be false to make the first and fourth statements true. But if we make C false in the third statement, it makes the third statement, the biconditional, false. So no matter what C is, one of the statements will turn out to be false. We signify this by placing an X over the T in the third statement – once we have made the other statements true, we can't make this statement true:

(A & B) & ~C   (D ∨ E) → ~B   (E ∨ F) ≡ C   F ∨ C
 T T T (T) TF   F F F (T) FT   F T T (X) F   T (T) F

We have a contradiction. If C is true, the first statement will be false; if C is false, the third statement will be false. Since there is no other combination of truth values that will make the first statement true, we can say definitively at this point that it is NOT possible to make all of these statements true at the same time. That means these statements are *inconsistent*.

Sometimes each statement can be made true in more than one way. In this case, you have to examine a row for the least number of ways to make any of the statements true. For instance:

$$A \equiv B \qquad (C \;\&\; B) \rightarrow \sim A$$

There are two ways to make a biconditional true and three ways to make a conditional true. We should use the method with the *fewest* possibilities. The two ways that a biconditional can be true are if its antecedent and consequent are both true, or if they are both false. So we can place those possibilities under the biconditional:

$$
\begin{array}{lll}
A \equiv B & (C \;\&\; B) \rightarrow \sim A & B \rightarrow C \\
T\,\textcircled{T}\,T & \textcircled{T} & \textcircled{T} \\
F\,\textcircled{T}\,F & \textcircled{T} & \textcircled{T}
\end{array}
$$

We can work out each line independently. A and B are both true in the first row;

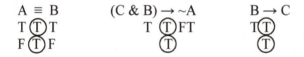

Now we have to assign a truth value to C. But we run into a problem. To make the 2nd statement true, since ~A is false, the conjunction would have to be false, so C would have to be false. But if C is false, the 3rd statement comes out false. If you make C true make the 3rd statement true, then that makes the 2nd statement false. In either case, both statements cannot be made true at the same time – so this row may be eliminated.

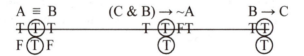

The first row does not show us that the statements are consistent. But, since we haven't yet considered ALL of the possibilities, we have to complete the second row. In it, A and B are both false, so we can fill in those truth values elsewhere

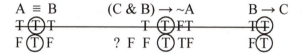

Regarding the 2nd statement, since B is false, C & B will be false whatever C is, so I put a ? under C. Then, since ~A is true, the biconditional will be true, so we can move to the last statement.

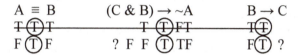

In the last statement, since B is false, it automatically makes the biconditional true – a biconditional with a false antecedent is always true. So I put another ? under the C to show that it doesn't matter what its truth value is. Thus, we have a truth-value assignment on which all of the statements are true. So the statements are consistent. The fact that they can't be made true on the first assignment means nothing. For consistency, all we need is a *single* truth value assignment on which all of the statements are true.

Here is a procedure for testing sets of statements with the indirect method:

1. Place a T under each statement.
2. Find a statement that can be made true in the fewest number of ways (look for conjunctions and biconditionals).
3. Make that statement true in all the ways that it can be made false.
4. Using those truth values, try to make all the statements true.
5. Stop when:
   a. You find the row you're looking for (all true statements). The set is **consistent**.
   b. You have eliminated every row. The set is **inconsistent**.

Validity

The indirect test for validity is the same basic operation as the indirect test for consistency, other than the difference in what row you're looking for. For validity, the row you're looking for is the row in which *the premises are all true while the conclusion is false*. So, consider this argument:

A → (D & F)   (D ≡ ~B) ∨ ~H   H ∨ J   /∴ A → B

We begin by setting up the condition we're looking for; in this case, true premises and a false conclusion:

A → (D & F)   (D ≡ ~B) ∨ ~H   H ∨ J   /∴ A → B
  Ⓣ   Ⓣ   Ⓣ   Ⓕ

Now we begin the process of examining possibilities. Since the premises must be true and the conclusion false, we have two places to look. In this case, though, the conclusion can be false in only one way, while all of the premises can be true in more than one way. The quickest way to test the argument is by starting with the conclusion (in general, it is easiest to start with the conclusion). A conditional is false only in the case where the antecedent is true and the consequent is false:

A → (D & F)   (D ≡ B) ∨ ~H   H ∨ J   /∴ A → B
  Ⓣ   Ⓣ   Ⓣ   T Ⓕ F

We can now put the value for A in the first statement:

A → (D & F)   (D ≡ B) ∨ ~H   H ∨ J   /∴ A → B
T Ⓣ   Ⓣ   Ⓣ   T Ⓕ F

Since the first statement is a conditional, with a true antecedent, it must have a true consequent (we want to make the *premises true*), so D and F both have to be true:

A → (D & F)   (D ≡ ~B) ∨ ~H   H ∨ J   /∴ A → B
T Ⓣ T T T   Ⓣ   Ⓣ   T Ⓕ F

We can place the values for D (from the first statement) and B (from the fourth statement) in the second statement:

A → (D & F)   (D ≡ B) ∨ ~H   H ∨ J   /∴ A → B
T Ⓣ T T T   T F Ⓣ   Ⓣ   T Ⓕ F

D ≡ ~B will be false, so to make the disjunction true, ~H will have to be true, which makes H false:

A → (D & F)   (D ≡ B) ∨ ~H   H ∨ J   /∴ A → B
                                              ◯

74.

T (T) T T T   T F F (T) T F   (T)   T F F

Since H is false, to make H ∨ J true, J will have to be true. Since J has not been assigned a truth value anywhere else, it can be made true:

A → (D & F)	(D ≡ B) ∨ ~H	H ∨ J	/∴ A → B
T (T) T T T	T F F (T) T F	F (T) T	T (F) F

Now, consider this row. We have constructed a situation in which the premises of the argument are true and the conclusion is false. Note again that it doesn't matter if there are any other such cases, nor how many there are. A single truth value assignment in which the premises are true and the conclusion is false is enough to prove an argument *invalid*.

Now, consider this slightly-revised argument:

A → (D & F)	(D ≡ ~B) ∨ ~H	H ∨ C	/∴ (A & B) → C
(T)	(T)	(T)	(F)

Again, we want to make the conclusion false, which can be done in only one way. This time, though, the conjunction A & B has to be true (so ANB both have to be true), and C has to be false:

A → (D & F)	(D ≡ ~B) ∨ ~H	H ∨ C	/∴ (A & B) → C
(T)	(T)	(T)	T T T (F) F

We can now put the value for A in the first statement:

A → (D & F)	(D ≡ ~B) ∨ ~H	H ∨ C	/∴ (A & B) → C
T (T)	(T)	(T)	T T T (F) F

Since the first statement is a conditional, with a true antecedent, it must have a true consequent (we want to make the *premises true*), so D and F both have to be true:

A → (D & F)	(D ≡ ~B) ∨ ~H	H ∨ C	/∴ (A & B) → C
T (T) T T T	(T)	(T)	T T T (F) F

We can place the values for D and ~B in the second statement:

A → (D & F)   (D ≡ ~B) ∨ ~H   H ∨ C   /∴ (A & B) → C
T Ⓣ T T T   T   F T Ⓣ   Ⓣ   T T T ⒻF

D ≡ ~B will be false, so to make the disjunction true, ~H will have to be true and H false:

A → (D & F)   (D ≡ ~B) ∨ ~H   H ∨ C   /∴ (A & B) → C
T Ⓣ T T T   T F F T ⓉTF   Ⓣ   T T T ⒻF

Now consider H ∨ C, the remaining premise. We know C is false, from the conclusion. We know H is false, from the second statement. So H ∨ C must be false. We signify this by drawing an X through the hypothetical T under the ∨, showing that it failed to be possible to make it true.

A → (D & F)   (D ≡ ~B) ∨ ~H   H ∨ C   /∴ (A & B) → C
T Ⓣ T T T   T F F T ⓉTF   F ⊗F   T T T ⒻF

This means that on the only truth value assignment on which the conclusion is false, one of the premises is also false. We can assert that there is NO case in which the premises are all true while the conclusion is false, so the argument is *valid*.

As with testing sets of statements for consistency, if none of the statements have only one truth value assignment on which it is true, you must examine all of the possibilities for the statement with the least number of ways it can be true. So, for instance:

(A & B) ≡ (A → C)   C ∨ B   ∴ A ≡ B

This conclusion can be made false in one of two ways; if A is true and B false, or if A is false and B is true. So we have to examine both of these possibilities:

(A & B) ≡ (A → C)   C ∨ B   ∴ A ≡ B
            Ⓣ   Ⓣ   T Ⓕ F
            Ⓣ   Ⓣ   F Ⓕ T

Taking the first case first, the values for A and B can be filled in in the first statement:

$(A \,\&\, B) \equiv (A \to C)$ $C \vee B$ $\therefore A \equiv B$

T F F (T)   T   T (F) F

         (T)   T   F (F) T

The conjunction, A & B will be false. To make the biconditional true, the consequent A → C must be false. Since we know A is true, C must be false:

$(A \,\&\, B) \equiv (A \to C)$ $C \vee B$ $\therefore A \equiv B$

T F F (T) T F F   T   T (F) F

         (T)   T   F (F) T

Since C is false and B is false, the disjunction C ∨ B will be false, so we can't make the second premise true. Place an X over the T.

$(A \,\&\, B) \equiv (A \to C)$ $C \vee B$ $\therefore A \equiv B$

T F F (T) T F F   F (X) F   T (F) F

         (T)   T   F (F) T

Since the premises on this row are not all true, it does not show the argument to be invalid. However, we cannot make a decision until we have examined *all* of the rows on which the conclusion is false. So we have to complete the second line. Here we know that A is false and B is true. Since B is true, the second statement will be true no matter what C is – C can be left blank for now:

$(A \,\&\, B) \equiv (A \to C)$ $C \vee B$ $\therefore A \equiv B$

T F F (T) T F F   F (X) F   T (F) F

         (T)   (T) T   F (F) T

We can place the values for A and B into the first statement and evaluated truth value of A & B:

$(A \,\&\, B) \equiv (A \to C)$ $C \vee B$ $\therefore A \equiv B$

T F F (T) T F F   F (X) F   T (F) F

F F T (T)   (T) T   F (F) T

The antecedent of the biconditional is false. In order to make the biconditional true, we have to make the consequent false. However, since A is false on this assignment, A → C will be true no matter what C is. So we cannot make the biconditional true, whether C is true or false. Place an X over the T in the first premise. It is helpful to place a ? under the C in both the 2nd and the 3rd premise to indicate that it doesn't matter:

$$(A \& B) \equiv (A \rightarrow C) \qquad C \vee B \qquad \therefore A \equiv B$$
$$\text{T F F } \text{①} \text{T F F} \qquad \text{F} \text{⊗} \text{F} \qquad \text{T } \text{Ⓕ} \text{F}$$
$$\text{F F T } \text{⊗} \text{F T ?} \qquad \text{?} \text{①} \text{T} \qquad \text{F } \text{Ⓕ} \text{T}$$

At this point we can say that we have examined *all* of the ways that the conclusion can be false (on any other assignment of truth values to A and B the conclusion would be true), and at least one premise was false on each of them. So we can now say that it is **impossible** to make this conclusion false while these premises are true, so the argument is *valid*.

Here is the procedure for determining the validity of arguments with the indirect method:

1. Place a T under each premise, and an F under the conclusion.
2. Make the conclusion false in all the ways that it can be made false.
3. Using those truth values, try to make all the premises true.
4. Stop when:
   a. You find the row you're looking for (true premises with a false conclusion). The argument is **invalid**.
   b. You have eliminated every row. The argument is **valid**.

Exercises

The Indirect Method for testing for consistency

Test the following sets of statements for consistency, using the indirect method. Be able to explain your results.

1. A & (B & ~C)   B ∨ (~A ∨ ~C)   (C ≡ A) & ~B
2. (A ∨ B) ≡ (B → ~C)   ((A & B) → C) ≡ B   (A & B) & ~C
3. (B & A) ≡ (A → C)   ~[(A & B) → C]   (B & C) → (A & B)
4. A → B   (B → C) & ~(A ∨ E)   D & (E ∨ B)   A ≡ E
5. A ≡ B   (A ≡ C) & (B ≡ ~D)   D → C   D & C

The Indirect Method for testing for validity

Test the following arguments for validity, using the indirect method. Be able to explain your results

1. $(B \& A) \equiv (A \rightarrow {\sim}C) \quad (A \vee B) \rightarrow {\sim}C \qquad \therefore (B \& C) \rightarrow (A \rightarrow B)$
2. $(A \vee B) \equiv (B \rightarrow {\sim}C) \quad ((A \& B) \rightarrow C) \equiv B \enspace \therefore (B \rightarrow A) \vee {\sim}C$
3. $(A \& C) \rightarrow B \quad {\sim}C \rightarrow D \quad (D \& B) \vee C \quad A \equiv D \qquad \therefore A \equiv B$
4. $A \rightarrow C \qquad B \vee D \qquad E \rightarrow A \quad (E \& C) \equiv B \quad D \rightarrow E \qquad \therefore A \& B$
5. $B \vee C$
    $C \rightarrow (D \& {\sim}E)$
    $(D \rightarrow E) \vee (A \& G)$
    $G \& H$
    $(H \& D) \rightarrow C$
    $\therefore A \equiv B$

Chapter 3: The Natural System of Deduction

3.1 – Introduction

Although the indirect truth table method is quite a powerful tool for analyzing statements and arguments, there are some even more powerful, useful, and elegant logical tools. In this chapter we will learn one of these tools, the **Natural Deduction Derivation System (ND)**. A **derivation system** is a proof system that begins with compound statements and uses a set of rules to derive other statements from the original set.

Derivations work in the opposite direction of truth tables. Truth tables work from the truth of simple statements to the truth of compound statements. Derivations start with compound statements and seek to derive or deduce information about the truths of the simple statements that make them up.

The word *derive* come from the Latin roots of *de-*, which means *from*, and rive, which is the same root as our word river, and means *to flow*. The word *deduce* comes from the Latin roots *de-* and *duce*, which is the root of our word duct, and also means *to flow*. In both cases, the references to the concept of validity. The truth of the conclusion *flows from* the truth of the premises – if the premises are true, then the conclusion must be true as well.

One of the fundamental aspects of a derivation system is that the system must be **truth-preserving**. This is a very abstract concept, but a truth-preserving system is **a system whose rules guarantee that, if you begin with true statements, everything that is derived from those statements will also be true**. If a derivation system is not truth-preserving, it is not trustworthy. That is, it cannot be trusted to yield true information from the original set. And if it cannot be trusted to yield true information, it cannot be relied upon to answer questions about the relationships between statements (or the world) correctly.

3.2 – The Rules of ND

A logical derivation system, again, is a system of rules for deriving information from an initial set of statements. The first thing to learn, then is the system of rules. The rules in this and all logical derivation systems are based directly on the truth tables for the different operators (so if you are not yet perfectly familiar with those truth tables, it would help you to spend some more time with them). The statements from which things are derived in a derivation system are always given as or assumed to be *true*. The rules of the system are based on information we can deduce about statement forms if we know (or assume) that they are true.

3.3 – The Rules of Inference

The rules of inference are derivation rules that tell us that from certain information, certain other information can be deduced or derived. They are in fact mini-arguments.

Conjunction Elimination (&E)[8]

The first derivation rule of ND is the "Conjunction Elimination" rule. Because the rules are truth-preserving, they tell us what can be deduced from true statements. So, suppose we are given the statement, A & B as *true* (that is, we are given the statement and told to assume it is true). Could we deduce anything about the truth values of the statements, A and B, which make up the conjunction? We could – we know that A and B have to *both* be true for the conjunction to be true. That means that, if we are given A & B, we can *derive* either A or B as true statements (remember, in a derivation system, we are working from the truth of compound statements to the truth of simple statements). We will symbolize this process like this:

1.	A & B	Given as true
2.	A	1, &E

OR

1.	A & B	Given as true
2.	B	1. & E

Derivations will always have this format: a line number on the left, a statement in the middle, and a *justification* on the right. Part of the truth-preservation requirements of derivation systems is that ***every line of a derivation must be justified***. A justification for a line is either "Given (as true)" (for statements in the initial set, which are always given as or assumed to be true), or one of the derivation rules, which are guaranteed to be truth

---

[8] This rule is sometimes referred to as "Simplification (Simp)."

preserving. In this way, we will always be sure that if we start with true statements, every derived statement will be true as well.

The rules will be given short-hand notations. The short-hand rule for "Conjunction Elimination" is "&E." This derivation rule, then, reads as **"from a given conjunction, either of the conjuncts may be derived on a subsequent line, citing '&E' as a justification."**

The formal presentation of &E is this:

$$\frac{p\ \&\ q}{\rightarrow p} \quad \text{OR} \quad \frac{p\ \&\ q}{\rightarrow q^9}$$

Disjunctive Syllogism (DS)

The rules of inference are mini-arguments (this is why they are called rules of *inference*). They follow from a general rule that says that any argument form that can be shown to be valid may be introduced as a rule in the system. This rule is based on the fact that if an argument form is valid, any argument that is an example of that form will be a valid argument. Furthermore, if the premises of a valid argument are true, then the conclusion is guaranteed to be true. So, if the premises of a valid argument form are given in a derivation, the conclusion of that argument form will be guaranteed to be true, so the form, including the conclusion may be introduced as a rule of derivation. The *Disjunctive Syllogism* is the first of this sort of rule to be introduced. The rule is:

1.	p ∨ q	Given
2.	~p	Given
3.	q	1,2, DS

Consider this as an argument (a *syllogism* is an argument with just 2 premises) with p ∨ q and ~p as the premises and q as the conclusion. Now consider an indirect truth table test of the argument:

$$\underline{p \lor q} \qquad \underline{\sim p} \qquad / \ q$$
$$\text{T ⑦F} \qquad \text{⊗T} \qquad Ⓕ$$

This argument is valid.

The best way to understand this rule is to think, if p ∨ q is true, then *either* p *or* q must be true. Then, if p is false (~p is true - that's given), then q

---

[9] The arrow → is the conditional arrow. It can be read here as "it follows that –."

must be true. This rule also works the other way: if p ∨ q is true, and q is false, then p must be true. The formal rule is:

$$
\begin{array}{c}
p \vee q \\
\underline{\sim p} \\
\rightarrow q
\end{array}
\qquad \text{OR} \qquad
\begin{array}{c}
p \vee q \\
\underline{\sim q} \\
\rightarrow p
\end{array}
$$

Conjunction Introduction (&I)

1.	p	Given
2.	q	Given
3.	p & q	1, 2 &I

This is a construction or introduction rule. It tells us that from any two statements given as true, we can derive the truth of the conjunction of the two statements. This is because if two statements are true, the conjunction of the two statements is necessarily true as well.

Modus Ponens (MP)

There are two rules in ND based on conditionals. The first is Modus Ponens (these rules were developed by Latin logicians and so have Latin names):

1.	p → q	Given
2.	p	Given
3.	q	1,2, MP

This rule is again based on an argument. If p implies q, and p is true, then q must be true.

Modus Tollens (MT)

Modus Tollens is the counter-part to Modus Ponens. It asserts this:

1.	p → q	Given
2.	~q	Given
3.	~p	1,2, MP

That is, if p → q is true and q (the consequent) is false, then p must also be false (otherwise p → q will be false).

To illustrate this, remember the indirect method: if you had this:

P → Q
? T F

Since the conditional is true, then, if Q is false, then P must be false to keep the conditional true. This is just what Modus Tollens says.

Two Common Conditional Derivation Errors:

Modus Ponens and Modus Tollens are often confused with the following two INVALID argument or rule forms:

Denying the Antecedent

1.	p → q	Given
2.	~p	Given
*3.	~q	1,2, ????

This is an INVALID form (the * at line 3 is an indication that this step is not a valid step). If the antecedent of a conditional is false, then the consequent can be either true or false. So you cannot derive anything from a conditional and the negation of the antecedent.

Affirming the consequent

1.	p → q	Given
2.	q	Given
*3.	p	1,2, ????

This is also an INVALID form. If the consequent is true, the antecedent could be either true or false. So you cannot derive anything from a conditional and the truth of the consequent.

Be careful not to confuse Modus Ponens or Modus Tollens with denying the antecedent or affirming the consequent.

Biconditional Modus Ponens (BMP)

There are two rules for biconditionals that follow the same general principles as those for conditionals. The first is Biconditional Modus Ponens:

1.	p ≡ q	Given
2.	p	Given
3.	q	1,2, BMP

The two parts of a true biconditional must have the same truth values. So if p ≡ q is true and p is true, then q must necessarily be true. This rule works the other way too; if p ≡ q is true and q is true, then p must be true.

Biconditional Modus Tollens (BMT)

1.	p ≡ q	Given
2.	~p	Given
3.	~q	1,2, MP

Remember, both sides of a true biconditional have to have the same truth value. So, if p ≡ q is true and p is false, q must necessarily be false. This rule works the other way too; if p ≡ q it is true, and q is false, then p must be false.

3.4 – Testing for Validity

The definition of validity for ND is,

> An argument is valid in ND if the conclusion can be derived from the premises.

Derivations in NS, then, are a procedure of deriving the conclusion from the premises. ND is based on the fact that, in deductive arguments, the conclusion does not provide any new information – it is a restatement or re-ordering of the information given in the premises. Derivations in ND are a process of deriving information from the premises to show that the information contained in the conclusion is already contained in the premises.[10]

---

[10] It is important to note that the definition of validity here is not an "if and only if" definition. If the conclusion *cannot* be derived from the premises, it doesn't prove that the argument is *invalid* (maybe you or I are just not smart enough to show how the conclusion follows from the premises). This makes ND weaker than TT as a proof system. It's strength is that it is more *natural*.

This procedure often involves two related steps. First is the step of *analysis*. "Analysis" means "to break down." It involves using the rules to break down the given statements into simpler statements. The second step is the step of *synthesis*. "Synthesis" means "to put together." In this step, we take the simpler statements we derived from the given set and try to build them back up into the form that the conclusion has.

An analogy for this process may be helpful.[11] Imagine the initial set of statements as an object constructed with Lego pieces. What you need to do is break these pieces apart and construct a new object with the pieces. You cannot add any new pieces to the set (but you don't necessarily need to use all of the pieces in the new object) – the procedure is just to take the original object apart and build a new object with the parts.

Let's begin with a simple derivation. Consider this argument:

A & B
A → C
/∴ C

To complete the derivation, we set up the premises of the argument as the given statements, and we place the conclusion to the right side of the last premise.

1.	A & B	Given (as true)	
2.	A → C	Given (as true)	/∴ C

The derivation or proof (in the future, I will refer to derivations as "proofs") proceeds in a fashion similar to that of TT. We place derived statements on subsequent lines, and we must provide a justification for every line of the proof. Once we have the conclusion on its own line with a justification we are finished. The first step is usually to look at the statements and see if there are any that can be broken down by the rules into simpler statement. The first statement is a conjunction. We can derive an A and/or a B from this statement by Conjunction Elimination. We don't necessarily need to derive both (but we can if we want); we only need to derive as much information as we need to complete the proof. Let's just derive the A for now:

---

[11] As is always the case with analogies, if this analogy helps you, please use it. If it does not help you, dispense with it immediately.

1.	A & B	Given	
2.	A → C	Given	/∴ C
3.	**A**	**1, &E**	

When new information is derived in a proof, it can be used along with the rules derive even more information. Now that we have the A, we can use it with A → C, and the rule Modus Ponens, to derive the C:

1.	A & B	Given	
2.	A → C	Given	/∴ C
3.	A	1, &E	
4.	**C**	**2, 3, MP**	

Note that the Modus Ponens justification requires citing TWO earlier lines; one which is the conditional (line 2) and the other which is the antecedent of the conditional (line 3).

Now we have a C on a justified line by itself. We have derived our conclusion from our premises, using the rules of the system. We have shown that if A & B and A → C are true, then C must be true as well. The proof is complete.

Now consider this argument:

A → D
D ≡ ~F
A
E → F
/ ∴ ~E

We will number the premises and place the conclusion (the statement to be derived) to the right of the last premise:

1.	A → D	
2.	D ≡ ~F	
3.	A	
4.	E → F	/∴~E

Now we begin the process. There are several ways to approach a proof. We can begin by breaking down statements that we can see can be broken down. Often the best way to do this is to look for conjunctions or single statement letters (which can be derived from conjunctions), because they can be used to break down other more complex statements. Here we have an A in statement 3. Can we derive anything (or break any statements down) with an A? We can: We know A is true and we know that A → D (line 1). Modus Ponens thus allows us to derive D:

1.	A → D	Given	
2.	D ≡ ~F	Given	
3.	A	Given	
4.	E → F	Given	/∴~E
5.	**D**	**1, 3 MP**	

Now we have a D. Can we use that to derive anything (or break down any other statements)? We can, using Biconditional Modus Ponens, with line 2:

1.	A → D	Given	
2.	D ≡ ~F	Given	
3.	A	Given	
4.	E → F	Given	/∴~E
5.	D	1, 3 MP	
6.	**~F**	**2, 5, BMP**[12]	

Now we have a ~F. Is there anything we can do with it? We have E → F in line 4. So we have a conditional and the negation of the consequent of the conditional. There is a rule that applies to this situation: Modus Tollens. It says that from a conditional and the negation of the consequent, we can derive the negation of the antecedent. So:

1.	A → D	Given	
2.	D ≡ ~F	Given	
3.	A	Given	
4.	E → F	Given	/∴~E
5.	D	1, 3 MP	
6.	~F	2, 5, BMP	
7.	**~E**	**4, 6, MT**	

---

[12] Note carefully that this is BMP, not BMT. We have not derived the negation of the antecedent with the negation of the consequent. We have derived the consequent (it just happens to be a negated statement) from the antecedent.

Now we have derived the conclusion, so we are finished. This proof was primarily analysis, since the conclusion came about from breaking down the premises. Synthesis is not always necessary in proofs.

Exercises

Derive the statements indicated. Be sure each step has a line number, a statement, and the justification.

A. 1.   A → B
    2.   A
    3.   B ≡ C   /∴ C

B. 1.   D ∨ E
    2.   ~D
    3.   E ≡ F   /∴ F

C. 1.   A → C
    2.   ~C
    3.   A ∨ B   /∴ B

D. 1.   C ∨ E
    2.   ~E
    3.   C → ~D
    4.   D ∨ B   /∴ B

E. 1.   C & D
    2.   C → E
    3.   D ≡ F
    4.   (E & F) → G   /∴ G

F. 1.   J → K
    2.   K ≡ L
    3.   L → M
    4.   M ≡ N
    5.   J   /∴ N

G. 1. $A \lor B$
    2. $\sim A$
    3. $B \rightarrow \sim C$
    4. <u>$D \equiv C$</u> $/ \therefore \sim D$

H. 1. $\sim A \lor B$
    2. $\sim B$
    3. $C \rightarrow A$
    4. <u>$C \lor D$</u> $/ \therefore D$

I. 1. $\sim A \lor \sim B$
    2. A
    3. $C \rightarrow B$
    4. <u>$D \equiv C$</u> $/ \therefore \sim D$

3.5 – The Rules of Replacement

Before beginning with the actual rules of replacement, I will introduce one more rule of inference, which is quite abstract, but used a lot with rules of replacement.

Disjunction Introduction (∨I)[13]

1.	p	Given
2.	p ∨ q	1, ∨I

This rule tells us that from any statement given as true, we can derive the disjunction of that statement with ANY other statement. This follows from the fact that a disjunction is true if either of the disjuncts is true. So, if a statement is given as true, the disjunction of that statement with any other statement (simple or compound) will be true. For instance, from the statement A given as true, we could derive any of the following statements:

A ∨ **B**
A ∨ (**B** & ~**C**)
A ∨ [(**F** ∨ **G**) & (~(**H** → **K**) ≡ (**L** & **M**))]

These statements may seem odd, but they follow directly from the rule that if either disjunct is true (in this case, A is true), the entire disjunction will be true. This rule is used very often in ND, so make sure to learn it and remember it.

Returning to rules of replacement, sometimes what is necessary in a proof is not breaking statements down or building new ones, but rearranging statements into different forms. Consider this proof:

1.	(A ∨ B) → C	Given
2.	~C	Given

There is only one move that can be made – a Modus Tollens on lines 1 and 2. That will give us:

1.	(A ∨ B) → C	Given
2.	~C	Given
3.	~(A ∨ B)	1,2 MT

---

[13] This rule is sometimes referred to as "Addition (Add)."

But now we have a problem. There is no rule or combination of rules that apply to ~(A ∨ B). It is not a disjunction – it is a negated disjunction – so DS does not apply to it. What logicians have done is recognize that certain statement forms are equivalent to certain other statement forms. Remember, equivalent statements are always true or false at the same time, so it does not change anything logically to replace a statement with an equivalent statement. That's what the replacement rules are.

There are a number of replacement rules. We have already encountered almost all of these rules as a result of showing in exercises that certain statement forms are equivalent to certain other ones.

We will write rules of replacement as

$p \equiv q$

The biconditional means "if and only if." The biconditional means that p and q are always true or false at the same time, which is the same as saying they're equivalent. A statement may always be replaced by an equivalent statement, and the replacement can go either direction.

Some of the rules of replacement seem obvious (and don't need to be cited), but help preserve the truth-preserving nature of the system:

Double Negation Elimination (~~E)

$\sim\sim p \equiv p$

This rule clarifies that 2 negations cancel each other out. If it helps you to use it, use it, but it is not necessary to use it.

Commutation (Comm)

$(p \mathbin{\&} q) \equiv (q \mathbin{\&} p)$
$(p \lor q) \equiv (q \lor p)$
$(p \equiv q) \equiv (q \equiv p)$

Commutation states that the order of the statements in conjunctions, disjunctions, and biconditionals doesn't affect the truth value of the statements. Once established, statements can usually be treated this way without explicitly citing this rule. NOTE: commutation does not apply to conditionals!

Association (Ass)

$$[(p \ \& \ q) \ \& \ r] \equiv [p \ \& \ (q \ \& \ r)]$$
$$[(p \lor q) \lor r] \equiv [p \lor (q \lor r)]$$

Association states that the grouping of conjunctions and disjunctions does not affect the truth value of the statements. Does association apply to biconditionals? We will leave this question to be answered by an exercise.

DeMorgans' Rules (DeM)

$$\sim(p \ \& \ q) \equiv (\sim p \lor \sim q)$$
$$\sim(p \lor q) \equiv (\sim p \ \& \ \sim q)$$

DeMorgan's rules (along with NCR, the next rule) are some of the most commonly used rules in logic. For the first form, $\sim(p \ \& \ q)$ has a $\sim$ outside of the parentheses. That $\sim$ doesn't allow us to work with what's inside the parentheses. We need a way to get rid of it. But, if we think through it, $\sim(p \ \& \ q)$ means that not both p and q are true. That means that at least one of them is false. So we are saying that p or q is false. We would translate "p or q it is false" as $\sim p \lor \sim q$ (remember, in logic, statements are always given as true – if we want to say a statement is false, we had a $\sim$ to it). This form is equivalent to the other form, and doesn't have a $\sim$ outside of parentheses. Since the statements are equivalent (you can use a truth table to demonstrate this to yourself if you want to), we can replace the one with the other – this is why these are called replacement rules.

For the second form, $\sim(p \lor q)$ means that neither p nor q are true. That means that they are both false, which can be translated as $\sim p \ \& \ \sim q$. Again, we can replace the statement that we can't use with a statement that we can use.

Negated Conditional Replacement (NCR)

$$\sim(p \rightarrow q) \equiv (p \ \& \ \sim q)$$

In this case we have a negated conditional $\sim(p \rightarrow q)$. That means that the conditional, $p \rightarrow q$, is false. We know that in a false conditional, p (the antecedent) is true and q (the consequent) is false. It would write that as $p \ \& \ \sim q$.

Material Implication (MI)

$(p \rightarrow q) \equiv (\sim p \vee q)$

This rule is based on the fact that in a true conditional, either the antecedent is false OR the consequent is true.

Transposition (Trans)

$(p \rightarrow q) \equiv (\sim q \rightarrow \sim p)$

This rule is based on Modus Tollens. If $p \rightarrow q$ is true, then if q is false, p must be false.

Material Equivalence (ME)

$(p \equiv q) \equiv [(p \rightarrow q) \,\&\, (q \rightarrow p)]$
$(p \equiv q) \equiv [(p \,\&\, q) \vee (\sim p \,\&\, \sim q)]$

The first ME rule is based on the meaning of the biconditional. $p \equiv q$ *means* that $p \rightarrow q$ and $q \rightarrow p$. The second ME rule is based on the truth table for biconditionals. If $p \equiv q$, then either p and q are both true, or p and q are both false.

Negated Biconditional Relacement (NBR)

Since we have a replacement rules for negated conditionals, we should have one for negated biconditionals as well – but it's fairly complicated! The simplest way is just to negate the 2 forms in the material equivalence equivalences:

$\sim(p \equiv q) \equiv \sim[(p \rightarrow q) \,\&\, (q \rightarrow p)]$
$\sim(p \equiv q) \equiv \sim[(p \,\&\, q) \vee (\sim p \,\&\, \sim q)]$

But those give us a negated conjunction and a negated disjunction. If you perform a DeMorgan's on each of those you end up with

$\sim(p \equiv q) \equiv [\sim(p \rightarrow q) \vee \sim(q \rightarrow p)]$
$\sim(p \equiv q) \equiv [\sim(p \,\&\, q) \,\&\, \sim(\sim p \,\&\, \sim q)]$

If we do in NCR on each of the statements in the first one, we get

$$\sim(p \equiv q) \equiv [(p \ \& \sim q) \lor (q \ \& \sim p)]$$

This last one is the truth table definition of biconditionals – they are false if p is true and q is false or if q is true and p is false. That's a lot of possibilities! NBR is not too common – if you see one, just figure out which of these forms is the one you need to do the next steps of the proof.

Exportation (Exp)

The proof of exportation will be shown in an exercise. It is simply cited here as a rule. Intuitively, if p implies (q implies r), then p and q should imply r.

$$[p \rightarrow (q \rightarrow r)] \equiv [(p \ \& \ q) \rightarrow r]$$

3.6 – The Reverse Strategy for Proofs

As proofs become more challenging, it is often difficult to see how to get started. In cases like this it is helpful to start at the end and work backwards (as before, if you find this process helpful, great; if you don't find it helpful, just start at the beginning and work your way down). That is, we can look at the conclusion and see where it will have to come from in the premises. For instance, using an earlier example:

1.	$A \rightarrow D$	Given	
2.	$D \equiv \sim F$	Given	
3.	A	Given	
4.	$E \rightarrow F$	Given	$/ \therefore \sim E$

Here, we have ~E as the conclusion. For this strategy we place the conclusion (to be derived) several lines down the page without a line number, since we don't know exactly how many lines we will need to get to it.

1.	$A \rightarrow D$	Given	
2.	$D \equiv \sim F$	Given	
3.	A	Given	
4.	$E \rightarrow F$	Given	$/ \therefore \sim E$

~E

96.

We can now look to see where we might derive a ~E from the premises. There is an E in premise 4. It is in the antecedent of a conditional. We can wonder, is there are rule that will allow us to derive the negation of the antecedent of a conditional? There is, Modus Tollens. So we can infer that we can derive the ~E if we can derive the negation of the consequent of this conditional, ~F. We place that on the line above the ~E:

1.	A → D	Given	
2.	D ≡ ~F	Given	
3.	A	Given	
4.	E → F	Given	/∴~E

~F
~E

Now we can consider where we could derive a ~F. There is a ~F in line 2. If we had a D, we could derive the ~F by Biconditional Modus Ponens. We can enter that information on the next previous line:

1.	A → D	Given	
2.	D ≡ ~F	Given	
3.	A	Given	
4.	E → F	Given	/∴~E

D
~F
~E

Now we can consider where we might derive a D. There is a D in line 1, which we could derive by Modus Ponens if we had an A. At this point, we can see that we have an A as a premise, on line 3. Since we now have all of the necessary steps, we can begin filling in the needed information, starting at the D. That came from lines 1 and 3 by Modus Ponens:

1.	A → D	Given	
2.	D ≡ ~F	Given	
3.	A	Given	
4.	E → F	Given	/∴~E
5.	**D**	**1, 3 MP**	
	~F		
	~E		

The ~F is derived from the D (line 5) and the biconditional in line 2, so we can complete the justification for that line:

1.	A → D	Given	
2.	D ≡ ~F	Given	
3.	A	Given	
4.	E → F	Given	/∴~E
5.	D	1, 3 MP	
6.	**~F**	**2, 5 BMP**	
	~E		

Finally, the ~E is derived from line 4 and the ~F in line 6, so we can complete that line:

1.	A → D	Given	
2.	D ≡ ~F	Given	
3.	A	Given	
4.	E → F	Given	/∴~E
5.	D	1,3 MP	
6.	~F	2, 5 BMP	
7.	**~E**	**4, 6 MT**	

Now we have derived our conclusion, have numbered all of our lines, and have completed our justifications, so the proof is complete.

This strategy is particularly helpful in eliminating unnecessary steps from proofs. Unnecessary steps do not affect the outcome of a proof, but they are inefficient and, well, unnecessary. Working backwards from the conclusion, while more abstract and complex, helps eliminate unnecessary work. It is also helpful when complicated replacements are necessary, because it is often difficult to see how the replacements must go to get from the premises to the conclusion.

Now consider this rather complicated argument:

$F \rightarrow B$
$B \equiv C$
$E \equiv \sim(F \vee G)$
$\sim(\sim A \ \& \sim F)$
$(C \vee D) \rightarrow E$
$\sim A$
$/\therefore \sim(G \ \& \ H)$

It is difficult to see on the surface where to begin the process of the proof. In cases like this, it is particularly helpful to use the reverse strategy. We begin by placing the conclusion further down the page:

1.	$F \rightarrow B$	Given
2.	$B \equiv C$	Given
3.	$E \equiv \sim(F \vee G)$	Given
4.	$\sim(\sim A \ \& \sim F)$	Given
5.	$(C \vee D) \rightarrow E$	Given
6.	$\sim A$	Given $/\therefore \sim(G \ \& \ H)$

$\sim(G \ \& \ H)$

We have a negated conjunction as our conclusion. Any time we have to work with a negated statement, we should think of DeMorgan's Rule to get the negations inside the brackets. By DeMorgans, this statement becomes:

1.	F → B	Given
2.	B ≡ C	Given
3.	E ≡ ~(F ∨ G)	Given
4.	~(~A & ~F)	Given
5.	(C ∨ D) → E	Given
6.	~A	Given /∴~(G & H)

~G ∨ ~H
~(G & H)

Now we have a disjunction to derive. Disjunctions are easy to derive: we only need to derive either of the disjuncts and use ∨I to add the other one. There is no H in the premises at all, so we can't derive that. But there is a G in line 3. So if we can derive a ~G, we can add the ~H by Disjunction Introduction:

1.	F → B	Given
2.	B ≡ C	Given
3.	E ≡ ~(F ∨ G)	Given
4.	~(~A & ~F)	Given
5.	(C ∨ D) → E	Given
6.	~A	Given /∴~(G & H)

~G
~G ∨ ~H
~(G & H)

Now we can look at premise 3 and see how we could derive a ~G from that premise. The right side of the biconditional in premise 3 is a negated disjunction. By DeMorgan's Rule again, it would be equivalent to (~F & ~G), and we could derive the ~G directly from that statement by a Conjunction Elimination. So if we can derive the ~(F ∨ G) from line 3, we can get the ~G. We can put this on our proof, using 2 steps:

1.	F → B	Given	
2.	B ≡ C	Given	
3.	E ≡ ~(F ∨ G)	Given	
4.	~(~A & ~F)	Given	
5.	(C ∨ D) → E	Given	
6.	A → B	Given	/∴~(G & H)

~(F ∨ G)
~F & ~G
~G
~G ∨ ~H
~(G & H)

We can derive the ~(F ∨ G) from line 3 with Biconditional Modus Ponens if we can derive the E:

1.	F → B	Given	
2.	B ≡ C	Given	
3.	E ≡ ~(F ∨ G)	Given	
4.	~(~A & ~F)	Given	
5.	(C ∨ D) → E	Given	
6.	~A	Given	/∴~(G & H)

E
~(F ∨ G)
~F & ~G
~G
~G ∨ ~H
~(G & H)

Now we have to derive an E. There is an E in line 5, as the consequent of a conditional. If we can derive the antecedent of the conditional, we can get the E by Modus Ponens:

101.

1.	F → B	Given	
2.	B ≡ C	Given	
3.	E ≡ ~(F ∨ G)	Given	
4.	~(~A & ~F)	Given	
5.	(C ∨ D) → E	Given	
6.	A → B	Given	/∴~(G & H)

C ∨ D
E
~(F ∨ G)
~F & ~G
~G
~G ∨ ~H
~(G & H)

Now we have to derive (C ∨ D). If we derive a C or a D we can get C ∨ D by Disjunction Introduction. There is no D in the premises, but there is a C in line 2:

1.	F → B	Given	
2.	B ≡ C	Given	
3.	E ≡ ~(F ∨ G)	Given	
4.	~(~A & ~F)	Given	
5.	(C ∨ D) → E	Given	
6.	~A	Given	/∴~(G & H)

C
(C ∨ D)
E
~(F ∨ G)
~F & ~G
~G
~G ∨ ~H
~(G & H)

Now we need to derive a C. We can derive a C from line 2 and Biconditional Modus Ponens, if we have a B:

1.	F → B	Given	
2.	B ≡ C	Given	
3.	E ≡ ~(F ∨ G)	Given	
4.	~(~A & ~F)	Given	
5.	(C ∨ D) → E	Given	
6.	~A	Given	/ ∴ ~(G & H)

B
C
(C ∨ D)
E
~(F ∨ G)
~F & ~G
~G
~G ∨ ~H
~(G & H)

Now we need to derive a B. We have F → B in line 1. If we could derive an F we could derive the B. The only lines we haven't considered so far are lines 4 and 6. Line 4 contains both an A and an F. It is a negated conjunction, so we can use DeMorgan's Rule to change it, we get A ∨ F. That, with ~A in line 6, will give us B.

1.	F → B	Given	
2.	B ≡ C	Given	
3.	E ≡ ~(F ∨ G)	Given	
4.	~(~A & ~F)	Given	
5.	(C ∨ D) → E	Given	
6.	~A	Given	/ ∴ ~(G & H)

A ∨ F
F
B
C
(C ∨ D)
E
~(F ∨ G)
~F & ~G
~G
~G ∨ ~H
~(G & H)

We have now completed the proof. We just have to complete the line numbers and the justifications:

1.	F → B	Given	
2.	B ≡ C	Given	
3.	E ≡ ~(F ∨ G)	Given	
4.	~(~A & ~F)	Given	
5.	(C ∨ D) → E	Given	
6.	~A	Given	/ ∴ ~(G & H)
7.	A ∨ F	4, DeM	
8.	F	6,7 DS	
9.	B	1,8 MP	
10.	C	2, 9 BMP	
11.	(C ∨ D)	10 ∨I	
12.	E	5, 11, MP	
13.	~(F ∨ G)	3, 12, BMP	
14.	~F & ~G	13, DeM	
15.	~G	14, &E	
16.	~G ∨ ~H	15, ∨I	
17.	~(G & H)	16, DeM	

The reverse strategy for proofs is easier for some people than others. Some people can work more easily from the beginning of the proof to the end. But some proofs (especially some yet to come) are so complex that it is the only feasible way to approach them. Furthermore, if, on a quiz or exam, you have all the correct steps listed, even without justifications, you will get 80% of the grade.

3.7 – Summary of ND Rules

Rules of Inference	
&E p & q OR p & q → p[14] → q	**&I** p q → p & q
∨I p → p ∨ q	**DS** p ∨ q OR p ∨ q ~p ~q → q → p
MP p → q p → q	**MT** p → q ~q → ~p
BMP p ≡ q OR p ≡ q p q → q → p	**BMT** p ≡ q OR p ≡ q ~q ~p → ~p → ~q

---

[14] In these rules, the symbol → stands for "it follows that…"

Rules of Replacement	
<u>DN</u> $\sim\sim p \equiv p$	**<u>DeM</u>** $\sim(p \lor q) \equiv (\sim p \ \& \ \sim q)$ $\sim(p \ \& \ q) \equiv (\sim p \lor \sim q)$
<u>MI</u> $(p \rightarrow q) \equiv (\sim p \lor q)$	**<u>NCR</u>** $\sim(p \rightarrow q) \equiv (p \ \& \ \sim q)$
<u>ME</u> $(p \equiv q) \equiv [(p \rightarrow q) \ \& \ (q \rightarrow p)]$ $(p \equiv q) \equiv [(p \ \& \ q) \lor (\sim p \ \& \ \sim q)]$	**<u>NBR</u>** $\sim(p \equiv q) \equiv \sim[(p \rightarrow q) \ \& \ (q \rightarrow p)]$ $\sim(p \equiv q) \equiv \sim[(p \ \& \ q) \lor (\sim p \ \& \ \sim q)]$ $\sim(p \equiv q) \equiv [(p \ \& \ \sim q) \lor (q \ \& \ \sim p)]$
<u>Trans</u> $(p \rightarrow q) \equiv (\sim q \rightarrow \sim p)$	**<u>Exp</u>** $[p \rightarrow (q \rightarrow r)] \equiv [(p \ \& \ q) \rightarrow r]$

Exercises

Part 1: Derive the following statements from the sets given. There are a lot of ∨Is in this set, watch for them!

A.   1. A → B
      2. ~B
      3. A ∨ (B ∨ D)   /∴ D

B.   1. D ≡ (B ∨ C)
      2. ~D
      3. B ∨ E
      4. C ∨ F   /∴ E & F

C.   1. M
      2. (M ∨ N) ≡ ~(P & Q)
      3. P & (R → Q)   /∴ ~R

D.   1. E
      2. F
      3. [(E ∨ M) & (F ∨ Q)] → G   /∴ G

E.   1. (B & C) ≡ (E & F)
      2. ~E
      3. B
      4. ~C → D   /∴ D

F.   1. [G ≡ (D & (E ∨ F))] ∨ B
      2. ~(B ∨ G)
      3. D & (H → (E ∨ F))   /∴ ~H

G.   1. (A → B) ≡ C
      2. ~C
      3. A → D
      4. E → B
      5. (D → B) ≡ F   /∴ ~F

H.   1. [(A ∨ B) → C] ≡ D
      2. ~(D ∨ A)   /∴ B

I.   1. [(A & B) ∨ (~B ∨ ~D)] → (E & F)
     2. <u>~E   /∴ ~(D → A)</u>

J.   1. A
     2. ~B
     3. C → (A → B)
     4. <u>C ∨ D   /∴ D</u>

K.   1. ~A
     2. (A → B) → (C → A)
     3. <u>C ∨ D   /∴ D</u>

L.   1. (~A ∨ B) → C
     2. D → (A→⊃ B)
     3. <u>~C   /∴ ~D</u>

M.   1. B → C
     2. ~(A → C)
     3. <u>D → (A → B)   /∴ ~D</u>

N.   1. (A & (B → C)) → D
     2. ~E → C
     3. <u>~(A → D)   /∴ E</u>

O.   1. ((A ∨ B) → C) → ((E & (F & G))
     2. B → C
     3. <u>~E   /∴ A</u>

3.8 – Advanced Proof Strategies

Conditional Proof (CP)

Sometimes there is not enough information provided in the premises to derive anything for certain. In such cases, it is often still possible to derive some things conditionally. That is, given the premises, and *assuming* other things to be true, we can derive certain information. However, in these cases, the derived information cannot be asserted for certain, but only *conditionally*. That is, it can only be asserted on the *condition* that the extra assumed information is true. Thus, we end up with a *conditional proof.*[15]

Here is a simple example of a conditional proof, which will serve as a rule:

$$A \rightarrow B$$
$$B \rightarrow C \qquad /\therefore A \rightarrow C$$

Note that the 2 premises are both conditionals. There is not an A or a B to break down the conditionals. But also note that the conclusion is a conditional as well. It doesn't state anything other than if A is true then C is true. So we only need to prove a conditional. Here's how it works:

1.	$A \rightarrow B$	Given
2.	$B \rightarrow C$	Given $\qquad /\therefore A \rightarrow C$
3.	$\quad A$	Assumption
4.	$\quad B$	1,3, MP
5.	$\quad C$	2,4, MP
6.	$A \rightarrow C$	3-5, CP

This proof illustrates several necessary aspects of a conditional proof. The first is *scope* of the conditional. In this proof the scope is the letters that are set off by lines. The idea of scope is part of the truth-preserving aspect of proofs. Given that certain things are true, certain other things follow. Anything derived from a set of statements given as true is said to fall within the *scope* of those statements. When we add an *assumption*, we are creating a new *scope*, because the added assumption was not given to us at the beginning of the proof and we cannot assert it as true unconditionally. We must indicate an added assumption and anything that is derived from that assumption with a secondary scope line inside the proof Notice on line 3 of

---

[15] In some texts and websites, Conditional Proof is called Conditional Introduction ($\rightarrow$ I).

our proof, we have added the assumption "A". We have not been given A as true; we are *assuming* it to be true. Now, anything we derive using A is only true IF A is true (which we are only *assuming*), and must be derived within the *scope* of that assumption. This is indicated by drawing a vertical line extending as far as we go on deriving things based on A.

The information derived from an added assumption must be treated carefully. The most important rule is that **none of the information derived within the scope of an added assumption can ever be used outside of the scope of the assumption**. So, in our example, we cannot use B or C to derive anything else in the proof outside of the inner line. They cannot be transferred to the main proof.

Nothing definite can ever be derived by means of an added assumption. Things can only be derived *conditionally*. Notice line 6 of the proof. What it asserts is a condition; IF A is true, then C is also true. We cannot assert the truth of C in the main proof, because its truth is only conditional – the condition is A's truth. We aren't given A as true – we had to assume it to be true. But note the conclusion: it is only a conditional. It only claims that A implies C. We *have* proven that, given the premises, A implies C, so we can enter that in the primary proof, and we have completed the proof. Note that the final line, A → C is not inside the secondary scope line. We have proved it non-conditionally. That is, given what we started with, we have proved it unconditionally.

The justification line for a conditional proof cites all of the lines in the sub-proof, including the initial assumption, and "CP", for "conditional proof."

Consider now this argument:

1.	A ≡ B	Given
2.	~B ∨ C	Given
3.	(C ∨ D) → ~(E ∨ F)	Given /∴ A → ~F

The indication that a conditional proof is required is a conclusion that is a form of conditional. Here we have A → ~F as the conclusion. The proof, then, involves showing that IF A is true, F is false. The first 3 statements are given as true, so we don't need scope lines for them. We next introduce the assumption and set up the secondary scope inside the main scope:

1.	A ≡ B	Given
2.	~B ∨ C	Given
3.	(C ∨ D) → ~(E ∨ F)	Given /∴ A → ~F
4.	⎸ A	Assumption

110.

Now that the scopes are set up, the proof proceeds as normal, taking care with the scope lines:

1.	A ≡ B	Given	
2.	~B ∨ C	Given	
3.	(C ∨ D) → ~(E ∨ F)	Given	/∴ A → ~F
4.	A	Assumption	
5.	B	1,4, BMP	
6.	C	2,5, DS	
7.	C ∨ D	6, ∨I	
8.	~(E ∨ F)	3,7, MP	
9.	~E & ~F	8, DeM	
10.	~F	9, &E	
11.	A → ~F	4-10, CP	

Regarding what to assume, we assumed the *antecedent* of the conclusion and, in line 10, we derived the *consequent* of the conclusion. Note again that the final line, A → ~F is not inside the scope line (it is not assumed or conditionally true; it is derived from the initial set of statements).

A conditional proof does not always need to be the final step of a proof. Sometimes they are necessary as part of a larger proof:

1.	A → B	Given	
2.	(B & A) → C	Given	
3.	(A → C) ≡ D	Given	/∴ D

This is a case where the reverse method works well. We have to derive D. We can get the D from line 3 using BMP if we can derive A → C. Since this is a conditional, if we assume the A and can derive the C, we can assert A → C in the main proof:

1.	A → B	Given	
2.	(B & A) → C	Given	
3.	(A → C) ≡ D	Given	/∴ D
4.	A	Assumption	
5.	B	1,4, MP	
6.	B & A	4,5, &I	
7.	C	2,6, MP	
8.	A → C	4-7, CP	

Note that we are now finished with our conditional proof. We have shown that A implies C, so we can assert this in the scope of the main proof. But we are not finished with the main proof, because we have not derived our conclusion. So we continue with the main proof:

1.	A → B	Given	
2.	(B & A) → C	Given	
3.	(A → C) ≡ D	Given	/∴ D ∨ E
4.	A	Assumption	
5.	B	1,4, MP	
6.	B & A	4,5, &I	
7.	C	2,6, MP	
8.	A → C	4-7, CP	
9.	D	3,8, BMP	

We have now derived the desired conclusion, so the proof is complete. In this case, the conditional proof is only one part of the overall proof.

Indirect Proof (IP)

Another proof strategy that uses sub-derivations is the indirect proof.[16] It is based on the facts that no consistent set of statements can yield any statement and its contradiction, and/or that any set of statements that yields both a statement and its contradiction is inconsistent. In this example, although the proof is simple without the indirect proof, the indirect proof can be used and demonstrated.

We start by writing out the premises and setting up the scope line. Our assumption is the negation of the conclusion. We write that at the top of the scope.

---

[16] In some texts and websites, Indirect Proof is called, variously, *Negation Introduction, Negation Elimination,* and/**or** *Reduction Ad Absurdum* ("reduction to absurdity" – because of a derived contradiction).

1.	A & B	Given
2.	A → C	Given /∴ C
3.	~C	Assumption (negation of Conclusion)

Now that we have the scope and the assumption set up, we start doing logic. The goal, again, is to find any contradiction – any statement and the negation of the same statement. Here's how it looks:

1.	A & B	Given
2.	A → C	Given /∴ C
3.	~C	Assumption
4.	A	1, Simp.
5.	~A	2, 3, MT
6.	A & ~A	*4, 5, &I[17]
7.	C	3-6, IP

The reasoning here, again, is: assume the *negation of the conclusion* (line 3); derive a contradiction (lines 4, 5), assert the (non-negation of the) conclusion. The justification is similar to conditional proofs: all the lines of the sub-proof, and the abbreviation IP.

Indirect proofs can also be used within a proof to demonstrate the truth of a needed statement:

1.	A → B	Given
2.	(C ∨ D) ∨ A	Given
3.	(C ∨ D) → A	Given
4.	B → F	Given /∴ F
5.	~B	Assumption
6.	~A	1,5, MT
7.	C ∨ D	2,6, DS
8.	A	3,7, MP
9.	A & ~A	*6, 8, &I
10.	B	5-8, IP
11.	F	4,9, MP

---

[17] This shows explicitly that a contradiction has occurred. Logicians have a hard time writing down a statement that is necessarily false, so they insist on marking this with an asterisk, to point out that this statement is not actually true.

In this case we needed to derive a B to get F. But there are no Bs that can be derived directly from the premises. But if we assume ~B, we can derive a contradiction, both A and ~A (we could also have derived the contradiction (C ∨ D) and ~(C ∨ D)). Since the addition of ~B to the premises allows a contradiction, it cannot be true. That means that B must be true, and so it can be declared on line 9, citing the Indirect Proof Rule as a justification.

Nested Proofs

To make matters more complicated, sometimes we must make assumptions within earlier assumptions. This creates a situation in which there are several levels of nested sub-derivations. Here is an example:

1.   A → (B → (C & D))   Given   /∴ A → (B → D)

It's hard to know how to get started here. The best way is to think through what the conclusion is saying. It's a conditional within a conditional. It says, ifAa is true then (if B is true, then C is true). We know how to do the outer conditional with conditional proof: we assume A and derive B → D. I'm going to set up the scope structure for this proof. The first step is:

1. A → (B → (C & D))   Given   /∴ A → (B → D)
2. | A   Assumption

           |
           |
           |
           | B → D
        A → (B → D)

This structure shows that, given the premise, if we assume A, and derive B implies D from it, we can assert the conclusion, B → D. B → D is a sub-conclusion – the conclusion of a sub proof. We know we can use conditional proof to derive conditional conclusions. So we can do another conditional proof to derive B → D. We have to set up another scope line inside the first scope line – this is a deeper scope – it is an assumption within an assumption. It will look like this:

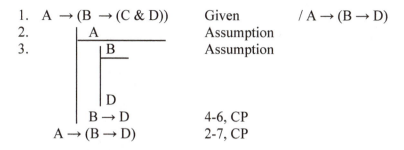

1. A → (B → (C & D))   Given   / A → (B → D)
2. | A
3. | B

                  | D
            | B → D   4-6, CP
        A → (B → D)   2-7, CP

Our new sub-proof says, if we assume B, we can derive D. That will give us B → D. Now we have to do the logic to make these assumptions and implications work out.

1. A → (B → (C & D))   Given   / A → (B → D)
2. | A   Assumption
3. | B   Assumption
4. | B → (C & D) 1,2, MP
5. | C & D   3,4, MP
6. | D   5, Simp.
7. | B → D   4-6, CP
8. A → (B → D)   2-7, CP

The initial assumption of A allowed us to derive (B → (C & D)). We did this inside the secondary assumption scope – that is fine – information can be brought from a higher scope into a lower scope (a more inside scope). The secondary assumption of B allowed us to derive C & D, from which we derived D. Thus, the secondary conditional proof showed that B → D (line 7), and the main conditional proof showed that A → (B → D) (line 8). Each of the 2 conditional proofs has a set of lines and "CP" as the justification.

Here is a more complicated example:

(A∨ B) → (C → D)
D ≡ (E & F)
~(E & F) ∨ J
∴ A → (C → J)

Note that the conclusion is a conditional within a conditional. This is the sign that the derivation will require nested conditional proofs (these cases are where working from the bottom up is particularly helpful):

1.	$(A \lor B) \rightarrow (C \rightarrow D)$	Given
2.	$D \equiv (E \& F)$	Given
3.	$\sim(E \& F) \lor J$	Given /∴ $A \rightarrow (C \rightarrow J)$
4.	A	Assumption
5.	$A \lor B$	4, ∨I
6.	$C \rightarrow D$	1,5, MP
7.	C	Assumption
8.	D	6,7, MP
9.	$E \& F$	2,8, BMP
10.	J	3,9, DS
11.	$C \rightarrow J$	7-10, CP
12.	$A \rightarrow (C \rightarrow J)$	4-11, CP

Here are the rules in abbreviated form:

Conditional and Indirect Proof Rules

CP or → I

  p (assumed)

  .

  .

  q (derived)

→ p → q

IP

  p (assumed)

  .

  .

  q & ~q* (derived contradiction)

→ ~p

Exercises

Conditional Proofs. Remember, assume the antecedent of the conclusion and derive the consequent of the conclusion.

A. Derive: **A → B**

1.	$A \rightarrow (D \lor H)$	Given
2.	$\sim A \lor \sim D$	Given
3.	$H \equiv (B \lor \sim A)$	Given

B. Derive **(A ∨ B) → D**

1. ~A & C   Given
2. (C & B) ≡ ~H   Given
3. (F ∨ N) → H   Given
4. ~F ≡ D   Given

C. Derive: **A → (B → C)**
   1. (A & B) → D   Given
   2. D ≡ ~G   Given
   3. G ∨ C   Given

D. Derive: **A → (B → (C → D))** This will require 3 nested proofs
   1. (A & B) → F   Given
   2. ~(C & G)   Given
   3. ~G ≡ (D ∨ ~F)   Given

E. Derive: **A ≡ B** Remember, p ≡ q means (p → q) & (q → p), so you'll have to do 2 conditional proofs and then create the biconditional out of them with ME.

   1. (A ∨ C) ≡ D   Given
   2. ~F → ~D   Given
   3. ~(F & G)   Given
   4. G ∨ B   Given
   5. ~(~B & G) → F   Given
   6. ~F ∨ A   Given

Indirect Proofs. Remember, assume the negation of the conclusion, derive any contradiction.

A. Derive: **A ∨ B**
   NOTE: There are often a number of different ways to derive contradictions in a proof.
   1. ~A → C   Given
   2. (~B ∨ F) ≡ D   Given
   3. (C & D) → A   Given

B. Derive: **~(B ≡ G)**
   NOTE: On this proof, the assumption may be made at the beginning, or later when it is directly called for.

1.	B & ~H	Given
2.	H ∨ (F ∨ I)	Given
3.	(~F & ~I) ∨ ~G	Given

C. Derive: **~[M & (N ∨ O)]**

1.	N → ~M	Given
2.	(O ∨ R) ≡ ~(H ∨ G)	Given
3.	M → H	Given

D. Derive: **A ∨ B**

1.	A ∨ ~(C → D)	Given
2.	F ≡ D	Given
3.	(C & ~F) → (G ∨ H)	Given
4.	H → F	Given
5.	~C ∨ ~G	Given

E. Derive **(B ∨ C) ∨ (B & ~C)**

1.	~(B ∨ C) ≡ (I → J)	Given
2.	(B → C) ∨ ~J	Given
3.	~I → (~J ≡ M)	Given
4.	I ∨ N	Given
5.	(M & N) → I	Given

3.9 – Theorems

The techniques of conditional and indirect proof are powerful logical tools. One of the main demonstrations of their power is their use in proving *theorems* in logic. The easiest way to think about theorems is to remember *tautologies*. A tautology, remember, is a statement that is necessarily true. A theorem is also a statement that is necessarily true. With respect to proofs, a theorem is a statement that can be proven true without reference to any other statement.[18] Beginning a theorem proof can be very strange and even unsettling, because you have no premises to begin with, you just start on a blank!

Let's begin with an example. Take the statement

$$((A \rightarrow B) \,\&\, A) \rightarrow B$$

This statement says that IF A implies B AND A is true, then it follows that B is true. You should be able to recognize that that statement will always be true; it doesn't matter what A and B stand for. So it's a tautology. We could prove that it's a tautology with a truth table, but we can also prove that it's a tautology with ND.

Notice that the form of the statement is a conditional (the main operator is $\rightarrow$). The conditional proof strategy always ends up with a conditional. A conditional proof works by assuming the antecedent of the conditional and showing that the conclusion follows. Since our statement is a conditional, we can begin directly by assuming the antecedent of the statement. Note: indirect proofs can also be used to prove theorems – some people find it easier.

1. $(A \rightarrow B) \,\&\, A$ Assumption

This may seem strange; we haven't been given any premises. But remember, we're only trying to prove that IF A $\rightarrow$ B AND A, then B will follow. So we assume the first part. Since this is an assumption, we have to set up scope lines:

---

[18] What this means regarding theorems is that they are not about the *meaning* of language at all, they are only about the *form* of the language (logic, in this case) and the relationships between different elements of the language (the logical operators, in this case).

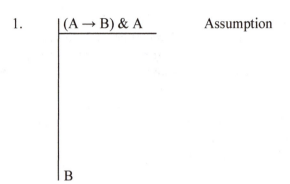

1.   (A → B) & A   Assumption

           B

Now we can begin the proof. The assumed statement is a conjunction, so we can break it down. The goal, again, is to derive a B from the statement we assumed.

1.	(A → B) & A	Assumption
2.	A → B	1, &E
3.	A	1, &E
4.	B	2,3 MP

So now we have shown that B does indeed follow from the first statement (IF it is true; but we aren't interested in that). But we're not finished. Our whole proof is inside scope lines, so we have only proven anything conditionally. But, in fact, that is all we were trying to prove. We wanted to prove that IF A → B AND A, then B. We have proved that. So we write, as line 5, *outside of the scope*, the theorem (line) that we set out to prove. The justification is just a conditional proof justification.

1.	(A → B) & A	Assumption
2.	A → B	1, &E
3.	A	1, &E
4.	B	2,3 MP
5.	((A → B) & A) → B	1-4 CP

3.10 – Proving Rules

One of the main uses of theorem proofs is to prove that the rules of ND are valid (i.e., they work). There is a neat (but rather abstract) method for doing this using conditional proof (it is worth noting here that any theorem proof may be accomplished using indirect proof as well). Take the well-used rule, DeMorgan's. We can ask, can we prove that it is true? In fact we can. The rule, from the list of replacement rules, is:

$\sim(p \ \& \ q) \equiv (\sim p \lor \sim q)$

As a regular statement this would read

$\sim(A \ \& \ B) \equiv (\sim A \lor \sim B)$

Now we want to prove that this statement is (necessarily) true. Remember, we are not being given this statement as a true premise; we have to prove that we can *derive* the statement from nothing! The first step is to remember the equivalence rule for biconditionals, which is that $p \equiv q$ means that $(p \to q) \ \& \ (q \to p)$. This is a conjunction of two conditionals. We know how to prove conditionals. If we can prove that $p \to q$ and that $q \to p$, then we can put the two conditionals together and derive the biconditional.

The strategy for proving equivalence rules, then, is
1. Prove that $p \to q$ (using conditional proof)
2. Prove that $q \to p$ (using conditional proof)
3. Join the two conditionals into the conjunction
    $(p \to q) \ \& \ (q \to p)$
4. Change the conjunction into a biconditional using ME.

The derivation will look like this

1.	p	Assumption
2.	.	Derived
3.	.	Derived
.	.	Derived
m.	q	Derived
n.	$p \to q$	1-*n*, CP
o.	q	Assumption
p.	.	Derived
.	.	Derived
r.	.	Derived
s.	p	Derived
t.	$q \to p$	*o-t*, CP
u.	$(p \to q) \ \& \ (q \to p)$	*n,t* &I
v.	$p \equiv q$	*u* ME

Notice again that we didn't prove anything about the truths of p and q. All we did is prove that IF p is true, THEN q is true and that IF q is true, then p is true. But that is all we need to prove to prove that p ≡ q is true, and that's all we're trying to prove.

One caveat is that if you're trying to prove a rule, you can't use the rule in the proof; you have to use other rules! This can sometimes be tricky, but there are always ways to use the other rules to get the same result. The three rules of DeM, MI, and NCR, can all be used to change between conjunctions, disjunctions, and conditionals, so are very useful. Just keep track of the signs!

~(p → q) + NCR ≡ (p & ~q)
~(p → q) + MI ≡ ~(~p ∨ q)
(p & ~q) + Dem ≡ ~(~p ∨ q)

Here is the complete proof for DeMorgan's.

Prove: **∼(A & B) ≡ (∼A ∨ ∼B)** (without using DeMorgan's)

1.	∼(A & B)	Assumption (Assume the antecedent of the first conditional)
2.	∼(A → ∼B)	1, NCR To prove any of DeMorgan's, MI, or NCR, you use the other 2 rules to change the form.
3.	∼A ∨ ∼B	2, MI
4.	∼(A & B) → (∼A ∨ ∼B)	1-3, CP NOTE that this line is NOT in the scope lines. This is the first half.
5.	∼A ∨ ∼B	Assumption (Assume the antecedent of the second conditional)
6.	A → ∼B	5, MI A helpful hint: once you figure out the steps for one transformation, the other one is just the same steps in reverse.
7.	∼(A & B)	6, NCR
8.	(∼A ∨ ∼B) → ∼(A & B)	5-8 CP NOTE that this line is NOT in the scope lines
9.	[∼(A & B)→(∼A ∨ ∼B)] & [(∼A ∨ ∼B)→∼(A & B)] 5,11 &I	
10.	**∼(A & B) ≡ (∼A ∨ ∼B)** **11, ME**	

Just to recap; we started with a bare assumption of the antecedent of the first conditional (line 1), then used replacement rules to transform it into another form (lines 2-4), then asserted the conditional (line 5, OUTSIDE of the scope). Then we assumed the antecedent of the second conditional (line 6), transformed it (lines 7-9), and asserted the conditional (line 10, OUTSIDE of the scope). Lines 11 and 12 are not in any scope; they're transformations of the two conditionals into the biconditional, which is the rule.

Theorem proofs are difficult; they require very abstract thinking. Just remember that theorems always use CP or IP, because you are not given any information to begin with. Also, remember that the statement to be proven is not given to begin with; it must be the end of the proof, derived from something else.

Exercises

NOTE: There are always a number of different strategies and proofs possible in theorem proofs. If your proof looks different than mine, that's okay.

Prove these tautologies:
1. $((A \to B) \& \sim B) \to \sim A$
2. $[(A \& (A \to B)) \& (B \to C)] \to C$
3. $(A \& B) \to (A \to B)$
4. $(A \& B) \to (A \equiv B)$ (create the 2 conditionals and join them with ME)
5. $(A \& \sim B) \to \sim (A \equiv B)$ (this is hard! Use NBR)

6. Prove the inference rule of Hypothetical Syllogism
        $((A \to B) \& (B \to C)) \to (A \to C)$
7. Prove Material Implication (without using the rule!)
        $(A \to B) \equiv (\sim A \lor B)$
8. Prove the rule of Transposition (without using the rule!)
        $(A \to B) \equiv (\sim B \to \sim A)$
9. Prove the rule of Exportation (without using the rule!)
        $(A \to (B \to C)) \equiv ((A \& B) \to C)$

Chapter 4: The Truth Tree Decision System

4.1 – Introduction

The Truth Tree system has some similarities to and some differences from Natural Deduction. Like ND, there are rules, line numbers and justifications (the justifications here work and look like the justifications of ND). The type of system, though, is different. While ND is a derivation system, TT is a *decision* system. I'll say more about this later. The way the system works is also different. We'll start by learning some rules, then start doing some proofs and discuss the system.

4.2 – The Rules of TT

Conjunction Elimination (&E)

The first rule of TT is the "Conjunction Elimination" rule (&E). It looks and works almost exactly like &E in ND.

1.	A & B✓	Given
2.	A	1, &E
3.	B	1. & E

The rule, then, reads, "**from a given conjunction, both of the conjuncts may be derived on subsequent lines, citing '&E' as a justification.**" After a statement has been derived (in TT, we say statements are decomposed or eliminated), we check it off, meaning that we don't have to refer to it anymore (this is a key difference from ND).

Disjunction Elimination (∨E)

Disjunction Elimination (∨E) starts to show the difference between ND and TT. When given a disjunction, A ∨ B, as true (remember, in logic, all statements are given as true), we will ask what can we determine about the truth values of A and B individually that will make A ∨ B true. The answer is, if *either* A *or* B is true then the disjunction is true. We want to know the conditions of the simpler statements that will make the compound statement true. For a disjunction, we will symbolize this information by making a branch (this is why this system is called the Truth *Tree* system):

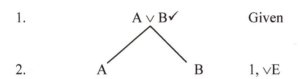

1.   A ∨ B✔   Given

2.   A   B   1, ∨E

This rule means that if the original statement is true, at least one of the two branches must be true. One way to think about this is that truth *flows* from the top of the tree to the bottom. Since A ∨ B is true, truth must flow through one of the branches.

Note that while conjunction uses two lines, disjunction elimination is done on a single line, but requires two branches.

4.3 – Truth Trees for Sets Of Statements, Part 1

Now that we have some basic rules, we can begin to construct truth trees for sets of statements. That is, given a set of statements, which we assume are true, we can use the rules to decompose them into the possible combinations of truth values for the simple statements that make them up. For instance, suppose we start with this set:

1.   ~A & ~B   Given
2.   A ∨ B   Given

The first two rules for working on a set of statements are these:

1. Start by eliminating statements that DON'T cause branches first (this keeps the tree simpler).
2. You must eliminate or decompose ALL statements that can be eliminated (whether in the original set or in any derived branch) before you are finished the derivation (with an exception that will be discussed shortly).

Taking our given set, the first procedural rule would instruct us to eliminate the conjunction first, because it will not cause any branches:

1.   ~A & ~B✔   Given
2.   A ∨ B   Given
3.   ~A   1, &E
4.   ~B   1, &E

Again, unlike ND, we check off statements when we have decomposed them – that's why they are called elimination rules.

Next, we will eliminate the disjunction:

1.	~A & ~B✓	Given
2.	A ∨ B✓	Given
3.	~A	1, &E
4.	~B	1, &E
5.	A B	2, ∨E

We have now eliminated both of our original statements. We have a fairly simple truth tree, with two branches. A branch starts with any letter at the bottom of the tree and proceeds upward all the way to the first statement on the list.

Note that if we read the left-most branch, we encounter both a ~A (line 3) and an A (line 5) on the branch. This is a **contradiction**. A contradiction says that a statement is both true and false, which is impossible. Truth cannot flow through that branch. We will CLOSE any branch on a truth tree that contains a contradiction. We close a branch on a truth tree by placing an X under it:

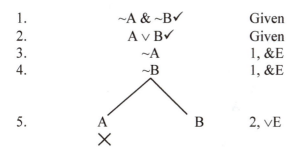

1.	~A & ~B✓	Given
2.	A ∨ B✓	Given
3.	~A	1, &E
4.	~B	1, &E
5.	A B	2, ∨E
	X	

Now, if we look at the right-most branch, there is both a B (line 5) and a ~B (line 4) on it, so it, too contains a contradiction, and must be closed:

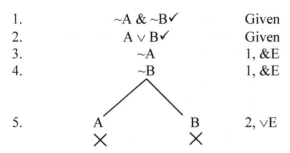

1.	~A & ~B✓		Given
2.	A ∨ B✓		Given
3.	~A		1, &E
4.	~B		1, &E
5.	A	B	2, ∨E

In this case, then, both (all) branches of the truth tree are closed. We will discuss the significance of this fact momentarily. Now consider this set of statements:

1.	A & B	Given
2.	A ∨ B	Given

To analyze this set, we begin, as before, with the non-branching statement:

1.	A & B✓	Given
2.	A ∨ B	Given
3.	A	1, &E
4.	B	1, &E

Now we eliminate the disjunction:

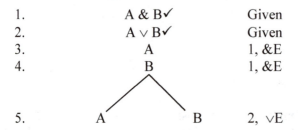

1.	A & B✓		Given
2.	A ∨ B✓		Given
3.	A		1, &E
4.	B		1, &E
5.	A	B	2, ∨E

There are no statements left to eliminate, so we can examine the branches. The left branch does NOT contain any contradictions. Neither does the right branch. We will identify a branch that doesn't contain any contradictions as an *open* branch and place a circle under it to indicate that it is open.

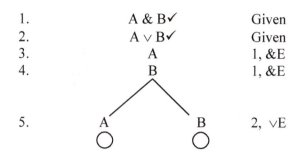

Truth Trees

1.	A & B✔		Given
2.	A ∨ B✔		Given
3.	A		1, &E
4.	B		1, &E
5.	A ○	B ○	2, ∨E

Once a truth tree is complete, according the rules, it will fall into one of two categories. Either *all* of the branches of the tree will be *closed* (like the first example) or *some* of the branches of the tree will be *open* (like the 2nd example). It is important to note that we are not concerned about whether *all* of the branches are *open*. The only issue is whether or not *all* of the branches are *closed*. We can now finalize the procedural rules for truth trees, clarifying the rule about when you can stop working on a truth tree:

Procedural Rules for Truth Tree Derivations:

1. Start by eliminating statements that DON'T cause branches first (this keeps the tree simpler).
2. All statement derivations must be entered at the end of EACH open branch in the tree *below* the statement being eliminated. (This is why eliminating non-branching statements first keeps the tree simpler). That is, when you eliminate a statement, you must trace it all the way down the tree and place it at the end of every open branch.
3. You must continue eliminating any compound statements on the truth tree until either
   a. all statements that contain an operator other than a single tilde are eliminated (checked off), or
   b. all of the branches of the tree are closed.

To illustrate rule #2, about branching, consider the following set of statements:

A & B, A ∨ ~B, ~A ∨ ~C

The first few lines of the truth tree for these statements will look like this:

1.	A & B✓	Given
2.	A ∨ B✓	Given
3.	~A ∨ ~C	Given
4.	A	1, &E
5.	B	1, &E
6.	A B	2, ∨E

We have eliminated the conjunction and one of the disjunctions. Neither branch of the tree is closed. But we are not done – there is still a statement that has not been eliminated. But there are two open branches. Where do we put the next information? This is where rule #2 comes in. The next elimination must be done *at the end of every open branch beneath it*. The disjunction will cause a split – this split must be done at the end of every (2 in this case) open branch below it – so it has to be done twice.

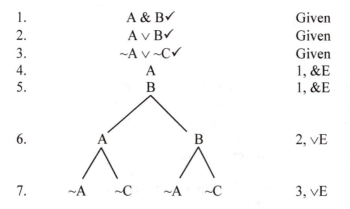

1.	A & B✓	Given
2.	A ∨ B✓	Given
3.	~A ∨ ~C✓	Given
4.	A	1, &E
5.	B	1, &E
6.	A B	2, ∨E
7.	~A ~C ~A ~C	3, ∨E

Now there are no more statements to be eliminated. We can examine the individual branches – there are four on this tree.

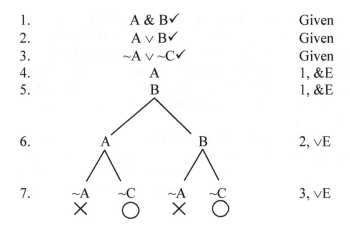

1.   A & B✓   Given
2.   A ∨ B✓   Given
3.   ~A ∨ ~C✓   Given
4.   A   1, &E
5.   B   1, &E

6.   A   B   2, ∨E

7.   ~A   ~C   ~A   ~C   3, ∨E

The left-most branch has an A and a ~A – it closes (remember, you have to trace branches all the way back to line 1 to look for contradictions). The second branch has no contradictions – it is open. The third branch has an A and a ~A – it closes. The fourth branch has no contradictions – it stays open.

Once rule 3 has been satisfied, we say the truth tree is **complete**. We can now provide some basic definitions about truth trees:

Complete truth tree: A truth tree is complete if and only if every statement that can be eliminated is eliminated, or on which every branch is closed.

Open truth tree: A truth tree is open if and only if it is complete and contains *at least one open* branch.

Closed truth tree: A truth tree is closed if and only if every branch is *closed*.

We can also now introduce the idea that is the foundation of the whole truth tree system:

> **A set of statements is logically *consistent* if and only if it (the set) has an open truth tree.**

That is, an *open* truth tree reveals that it is possible for all of the statements to be true at the same time (and actually gives you a set of truth values that will make the statements true). This is just the definition of a consistent set of statements. On the other hand, a *closed* truth *tree* (not a closed branch) reveals that it is not possible for the statements all to be true at the same time. This is the definition of an inconsistent set of statements. Furthermore, any open branch on a truth tree will provide a set of truth values (the truth values of the simple statements on the open branch) on which all of the statements are true.

One way to imagine this idea is to think that there's a "bucket of truth" on the top of the tree. The question is, can truth flow all of the way through the tree? If it can (a branch is open), the tree is open and the set is consistent. If not (all of the branches are closed), the tree is closed and the set is inconsistent.

4.4 – More Elimination Rules

Conditional Elimination (→E)

For conditional elimination, remember MI from ND.

$$(p \rightarrow q) \equiv (\sim p \lor q)$$

If a conditional is true, then *either* the antecedent is false *or* the consequent is true. So the conditional becomes a disjunction:

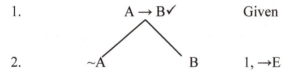

1.   A → B✓   Given

2.   ~A   B   1, →E

The left branch and this tree illustrates a complicated matter in logic. The A in line one does not have a ~ – but the A in line 2 does have a ~. This means that *whatever* the truth value of A in the first statement, it must have the *opposite* truth value in the derived statement. Since it was a positive A in the conditional, it is written as ~A on the elimination line. If it were a ~A in the conditional, it would become the negation of ~A in the elimination line, which would be, technically, ~~A, but, we know that 2 tildes cancel each other out, so it would be just A. Similarly, if the statement was (A ∨ B) → C, the left branch would get ~(A ∨ B) and the right branch would get C. If the statement was ~(A ∨ B) → C, the left branch would get (A ∨ B) and the right branch would get C.

Biconditional Elimination (≡E)

For biconditional elimination, remember when biconditionals are true. A biconditional is true when the two statements that make it up are both true OR when the two statements that make it up are both false. So, if a biconditional is given as true, we know that one of those two situations must hold. We can then write:

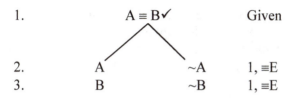

1.		A ≡ B✓	Given
2.	A	~A	1, ≡E
3.	B	~B	1, ≡E

We read this as, if the biconditional is true, either A and B are true (lines 2 and 3, left branch) OR A and B are false (lines 2 and 3, right branch).

Exercises

Are the following sets of statements consistent or inconsistent? Use a truth tree to evaluate them. Explain whether the tree is open or closed, and why, and whether the set is consistent or inconsistent based on the tree, and why.

A. 1.   A & B   Given
    2.   C & D   Given
    3.   ~A ∨ ~D   Given

B. 1.   A & B   Given
    2.   A → C   Given
    3.   B → D   Given
    4.   ~C ∨ ~D   Given

C. 1.   F → G   Given
    2.   G ≡ ~H   Given
    3.   ~H ∨ ~F   Given

D. 1.   M & N   Given
    2.   N → ~O   Given
    3.   M → ~P   Given
    4.   ~O ∨ ~P   Given

E. 1.   R & S   Given
    2.   R ≡ T   Given
    3.   T → S   Given

4.5 – Negation Elimination Rules

The elimination rules we have so far will allow us to eliminate all of the basic statement forms, so long as they are not negated. But these rules do not apply to negated statements, such as ~(A & B). We need to expand our set of elimination rules to apply to negated statements as well, which we now do:

Double Negation Elimination (~~E)

The double-negation elimination rule is a safety rule. In carrying out the following rules, a negated statement often has to be negated. Officially, what results is a double negation. A double negation functions in logic much like a double negation functions in algebra – the two negations cancel each other. If you can work out the cancellation correctly without using the double negation step, you may, but it is safer to include the double-negation step. The rule is:

1.   ~~A✓   Given
2.   A   1, ~~E

Negated Conjunction Elimination (~&E or DeM)

For negation rules, think of the replacement rules from ND. If ~(A & B) is true, then, by DeMorgan's, you know that ~A ∨ ~B. We now have a disjunction, and the rule for a negated conjunction will look like the rule for a disjunction:

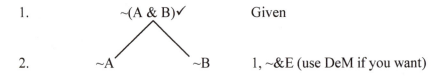

1.   ~(A & B)✓   Given

2.   ~A   ~B   1, ~&E (use DeM if you want)

Negated Disjunction Elimination (~∨E or DeM)

A negated disjunction, ~(A ∨ B), by DeMorgan's, is ~A & ~B. The rule will thus look similar to the rule for conjunction elimination:

1.	~(A ∨ B)✓	Given
2.	~A	1, ~∨E (use DeM if you want)
3.	~B	1, ~∨E

Negated Conditional Elimination (~→E or NCR)

For conditional elimination, use NCR. ~(A → B) becomes A & ~B. Thus, the rule for negated conditional elimination will look like conjunction elimination, for the condition that A is true and B is false:

1.	~(A → B)✓	Given
2.	A	1, ~→E (use NCR if you want)
3.	~B	1, ~→E

Negated Biconditional Elimination (~≡E or NBR)

Biconditionals are always difficult. Remember NBR:

$$\sim(A \equiv B) \equiv [(A \ \& \sim B) \lor (\sim A \ \& \ B)]$$

A biconditional is false when the antecedent is true and the consequent is false, *or* when the antecedent is false and the consequent is true. It might be helpful to write the intermediate steps:

1.	~(A ≡ B)✓	Given
2.	(A & ~B) ∨ (~A & B)	1, NBR

3.	A & ~B		~A & B	1, ∨E
4.	A		~A	3, &E
5.	~B		B	3, &E

The official form of the rule is just:

1.   ~(A ≡ B)✓   Given

2.   A   ~A   1, ~≡E (use NBR if you want)
3.   ~B   B   1, ~≡E

Here is a summary of all of the truth tree elimination rules:

Truth Tree Elimination Rules:

Exercises

Use truth trees to determine whether the following sets of statements are consistent or not. For each, explain how the truth tree is the answer to the consistency question.

A. A & B	(A ∨ B) ∨ C	~C	
B. A → (B & C)	C → D	D ≡ ~A	
C. A & (B ∨ C)	C → ~(A ∨ D)	~(B → ~E)	~(E ≡ ~C)
D. F ≡ ~(D & ~E)	(F & H) & ~G	D ∨ ~H	H → E
E. P ≡ ~(Q ∨ R)	(~P ∨ Q) → ~U	~(P & U)	U ≡ ~W

4.6 – Truth Trees for Sets Of Statements, Part 2

We know the relationship between truth trees and consistency. We will now put that knowledge to work to test statements and sets of statements for other logical properties as well.

Testing For Logical Falsehood

A logically false statement is a statement that is false under every truth value assignment. Can we express this concept in terms of the concept of consistency? It may seem odd to use a truth tree, which is designed to test sets of statements, to test a single statement. But the truth tree test, remember, is designed to test any set of statements for consistency. It is possible to have a set consisting of a single statement.

What would it mean for a single statement to be *consistent*? As with any set, it would just mean that there is at least one truth value assignment on which that statement is true. What would it mean for a single statement to be *inconsistent*? It would mean that there are NO truth value assignments on which that statement is true. But if a statement is false under every truth value assignment, then the statement is logically false. So we can say that a statement is logically false if and only if it is inconsistent. With respect to truth trees, any inconsistent set of statements will have a closed truth tree. So a single inconsistent statement will have a closed truth tree. We can test for logically false statements using a truth tree then, using this definition:

A statement is logically false if and only if it has a closed truth tree.

For example:

1.	$(A \lor B) \& (\sim A \& \sim B)$✓	Given
2.	$A \lor B$✓	1, &E
3.	$\sim A \& \sim B$✓	1, &E
4.	$\sim A$	3, &E
5.	$\sim B$	3, &E

6.	A	B	2, $\lor$E
	✕	✕	

Both branches of this tree are closed, so it is not possible to make the statement true, so it is both inconsistent and logically false.

Testing for Logical Truth

Testing single statements for being logically true is similar to, but more complex than, testing them for being logically false. The immediate intuition is that if a statement has all open branches, the statement must be logically true. But this is false. Consider the truth tree for this statement:

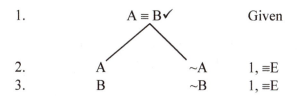

This is the truth tree for a basic biconditional. Note that there are no closed branches on this tree, and that the tree is complete. But a simple biconditional statement is not logically true. So our intuition here leads us astray. We have to think more about the relationship between consistency and logical truth.

We know that a logically true statement is true on every truth value assignment. The question is, can we relate this situation to the concept of consistency? It is tricky, but can be done. Consider this. If a statement is negated, it will have the opposite truth value than it did before it was negated, in all cases. What would happen to a logically true statement if it was negated? Then, rather than being true in every case, it would be false in every case – it would be a logically false statement. And, as we have just learned, we can test for logically false statements with truth trees. From this information, we gain the following definition:

> **A statement is a logically true if and only if its *negation* has a closed truth tree**.

For instance, for the statement, $[(A \rightarrow B) \rightarrow (\sim A \vee B)]$, we would test the negation;

$\sim[(A \rightarrow B) \rightarrow (\sim A \vee B)]$:

1.	~[(A → B) → (~A ∨ B)]✓	Given
2.	A → B✓	1, ~→E
3.	~(~A ∨ B)✓	1, ~→E
4.	~~A	3, ~∨E
5.	~B	3, ~∨E
6.	A	4, ~~E

| 7. | ~A   B | 2, →E |
| | ✗   ✗ | |

The truth tree is complete and has all closed branches. This means that the *statement being tested* is false on every truth value assignment, or inconsistent, or logically false. This means that the *original* (non-negated) statement is true on every truth value assignment, or logically true.

Note that "consistent" and "logically true" do not mean the same thing. A statement needs be true on only *one* truth value assignment to be consistent. A statement must be true on *every* truth value assignment to be logically true.

Testing For Logical Equivalence

Truth tables can be used to test pairs of statements for equivalence. The process, however, is tricky and requires some abstract thinking.

If two statements are equivalent, then they always have the same truth value. One of our basic operators has the characteristic that it will be true if both parts of it have the same truth value, and false if both parts of it have different truth values.

Here is the truth table for that operator: can you identify it?

p	q	p ? q
T	T	T
T	F	F
F	T	F
F	F	T

This is the truth table for the *biconditional*. Now consider what would happen if we put two equivalent statements together as a biconditional. What property would the biconditional have? It would be true in every case, because the two (equivalent) statements would always have the same truth value (either both true together or both false together). So the biconditional formed of two equivalent statements would be logically true.

140.

We know how to test for logically true statements using truth trees: we see if the negation of the statement is consistent. That means that to test whether two statements are equivalent we can test *the negation of the biconditional composed of the two statements* for consistency. For a definition, we get:

Two statements are logically equivalent if and only if the *negation* of the *biconditional* composed of the two statements has a *closed* truth tree.

This test must be done in steps:

1. Combine the two statements into a biconditional.
2. Negate the biconditional.
3. Test the negated biconditional for consistency.
4. If the negated biconditional is inconsistent, the two statements are logically equivalent; if the negated biconditional is consistent, the two statements are not logically equivalent.

For example, consider two statements we know are equivalent, ~(A ∨ B) and (~A & ~B). We combine them together into a biconditional;

$$[\sim(A \lor B) \equiv (\sim A \mathbin{\&} \sim B)]$$

Next, we negate the biconditional:

$$\sim[\sim(A \lor B) \equiv (\sim A \mathbin{\&} \sim B)]$$

Then we test the biconditional with a truth tree:

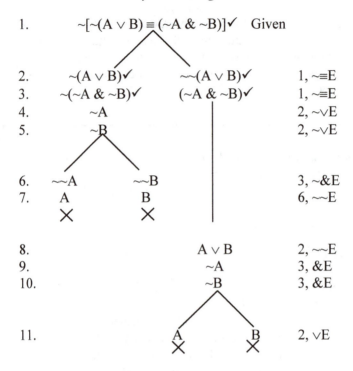

1. $\sim[\sim(A \lor B) \equiv (\sim A \,\&\, \sim B)]\checkmark$ Given

2. $\sim(A \lor B)\checkmark$ | $\sim\sim(A \lor B)\checkmark$ | $1, \sim\equiv E$
3. $\sim(\sim A \,\&\, \sim B)\checkmark$ | $(\sim A \,\&\, \sim B)\checkmark$ | $1, \sim\equiv E$
4. $\sim A$ | | $2, \sim\lor E$
5. $\sim B$ | | $2, \sim\lor E$

6. $\sim\sim A$ | $\sim\sim B$ | | $3, \sim\&E$
7. A | B | | $6, \sim\sim E$
   $\times$ | $\times$

8. | | $A \lor B$ | $2, \sim\sim E$
9. | | $\sim A$ | $3, \&E$
10. | | $\sim B$ | $3, \&E$

11. | | A B | $2, \lor E$
    | | $\times$ $\times$

The truth tree for the negated biconditional is closed. This means:

1. The *negated biconditional* is logically false (it is never true), so
2. the (non-negated) *biconditional* is logically true (it is always true), so
3. the two statements *always* have the same truth values, so
4. the two statements are *equivalent*.

Now let's look at a truth tree for two non-equivalent statements, $(A \rightarrow B)$ and $(B \rightarrow A)$.

We combine them into a biconditional:

$[(A \rightarrow B) \equiv (B \rightarrow A)]$

We negate the biconditional:

$\sim[(A \rightarrow B) \equiv (B \rightarrow A)]$

We construct a truth tree for the negated biconditional:

142.

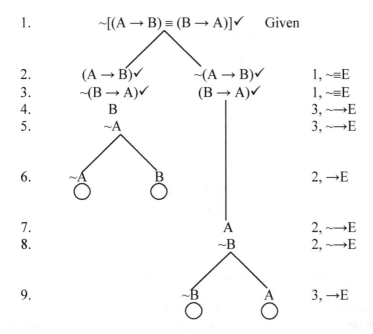

1.   ~[(A → B) ≡ (B → A)]✓   Given

2.	(A → B)✓ ~(A → B)✓	1, ~≡E
3.	~(B → A)✓ (B → A)✓	1, ~≡E
4.	B	3, ~→E
5.	~A	3, ~→E
6.	~A B	2, →E
7.	A	2, ~→E
8.	~B	2, ~→E
9.	~B A	3, →E

This negated biconditional has an open tree. Note carefully that although this tree has ALL open branches, it is not the property of having all open branches that makes it open; it is the property of having SOME – at least one – open branches that makes it open. Technically, we could have stopped completing the tree at the left-most branch, since as soon as we have a single open branch with no more statements to eliminate on that branch, the tree is an open tree. An open tree here means (thinking backwards through the process):

1. the *negated biconditional* is *not* logically false (it is sometimes true), so
2. the (non-negated) *biconditional* is *not* logically true (it is sometimes false), so
3. the two statements *do not always* have the same truth values, so
4. the two statements are *not equivalent*.

Exercises

<u>Testing for Logical Truth</u>
Use truth trees to determine whether the following statements are logically true, logically false, or neither:

A.   ~(W & E) ∨ (S ∨ N)
B.   (A ≡ B) & (A & ~B)

C. $(C \lor D) \to \sim(\sim C \to D)$
D. $[A \& (B \lor C)] \& [(\sim A \lor \sim B) \& \sim C]$
E. $[B \& (F \lor C)] \to [(B \& F) \lor (B \& C)]$

Testing for Logical Equivalence
Use truth trees to determine whether the following statements are equivalent or not:

A. $A \to B$ $\sim A \to \sim B$
B. $A \to B$ $\sim B \to \sim A$
C. $[B \& (F \lor C)]$ $[(B \& F) \lor (B \& C)]$
D. $[P \to (Q \to R)]$ $[(P \& Q) \to R]$
E. $[A \to (B \to (C \to D))]$ $[\sim A \lor (B \lor (\sim D \to \sim C))]$

4.7 Testing Arguments for Validity

Although the properties of logical truth, falsehood, consistency, and equivalence are interesting to logicians, the point of logic in the long run is to test arguments for validity. We can use truth trees to test arguments for validity as well. To do so, as we have been doing, we have to express the notion of validity in terms of consistency.

A valid argument is one in which there are no truth value assignments on which the premises are all true and the conclusion is false. But consistency can only test whether a set of statements can all be true. As before, we have to think about how we can express the idea of validity in terms of a set of statements we can test for consistency. We want to test whether the premises can all be true, so they're already in the form that we want them to be. But the test case is the one in which the conclusion is false. Is there something we can do to the conclusion so that we can look at it in terms of truth? There is – we can *negate* it. If the conclusion is false, the negation of the conclusion will be true.

In order to test an argument for validity, then, we can test the set of statements that is made up of the premises plus the *negation of the conclusion*. If we can make that set all true (i.e., the set is *consistent*), then we have made the premises true while the conclusion is false, and so we have shown the argument to be invalid. On the other hand, if we cannot make this set all true (i.e., the set is *inconsistent*), that means that we cannot make the premises true while the negation of the conclusion is true, or, we cannot make the premises true while the (non-negated) conclusion is false, so we will have shown the argument to be valid. And we can test a set of statements for consistency with a truth tree. We thus get the following rule for testing arguments:

> **An argument is valid if and only if the truth tree of the set composed of the premises plus the negation of the conclusion is *closed*.**

For instance, consider the following argument, which we have proven before to be valid;

$$A \rightarrow B$$
$$B \rightarrow C$$
$$\therefore A \rightarrow C$$

To test this argument, we combine the two premises with the negation of the conclusion:

$$A \rightarrow B$$
$$B \rightarrow C$$
$$\sim(A \rightarrow C)$$

We now test this set of statements for consistency:

1.	$A \rightarrow B\checkmark$	Given
2.	$B \rightarrow C\checkmark$	Given
3.	$\sim(A \rightarrow C)\checkmark$	Given
4.	A	3, $\sim\rightarrow$E
5.	$\sim C$	3, $\sim\rightarrow$E
6.		

7.	$\sim A$ B	1, $\rightarrow$E
8.	$\sim B$ C	2, $\rightarrow$E

The truth tree is complete, and it has all closed branches. This means (thinking backwards through the process):

1. The set of statements consisting of the premises and the *negation* of the conclusion is *inconsistent*. That is,
2. The premises and the *negation* of the conclusion *cannot* all be made *true* at the same time. So,
3. The premises *cannot* be made *true* while the (non-negated) conclusion is *false*. So,
4. The argument is *valid*.

Now consider this slightly-revised argument:

A → B
B → C
∴ A → ~C

Again, we want to test the set consisting of the premises and the negation of the conclusion;

A → B
B → C
~(A → ~C)

We test this set using a truth-tree:

1.	A → B✓	Given
2.	B → C✓	Given
3.	~(A → ~C)✓	Given
4.	A	3, ~→E
5.	~~C	3, ~→E
6.	C	5, ~~E

7.	~A B	1, →E
8.	~B C	2, →E

The truth tree is complete, and it has an open branch. This means (thinking backwards through the process):

1. The set of statements consisting of the premises and the negation of the conclusion is *consistent*. That is,

2. The premises and the negation of the conclusion *can* all be made *true* at the same time. So,
3. The premises *can* be made *true* while the (non-negated) conclusion is *false*. So,
4. The argument is *invalid*.

Exercises

<u>Testing for Validity</u>
Use truth trees to test the following arguments for validity.

A. A → ~B   C → ~D   A ∨ C   /∴ ~B ∨ ~D
B. A → ~(B ∨ C) D ≡ C   (D ∨ F) → A   /∴ ~A ∨ B
C. D ∨ B   (B & A) ≡ C   ~C ∨ D   /∴ A → D
D. (A & B) ∨ C   C ≡ ~(D ∨ E) (A → D) → (B ∨ ~C) /∴ A & B
E. (F &I) → J   ~(H ≡ J)   ~(I → F) & H   /∴ (~F & G) & H

Chapter 5: Predicate Logic

5.1 – Single-Place Predicates

In this chapter we will consider a new way of symbolizing statements. Consider the following argument:

All cats are mammals
All mammals have hair
Therefore, all cats have hair

Whether or not it is sound, this argument seems to be valid. If we were to symbolize this argument In Sentential Logic and in Natural Deduction, we would have to symbolize the first statement with a single capital letter, like *C*; we would have to symbolize the second statement and with a different capital letter, like *M*, and we would have to symbolize the third statement with yet another capital letter, like *H*.

The argument then, would look something like

C
M
∴H

This symbolized argument, however, is not a valid argument form. This situation reveals a limitation of SL and ND. We need to develop some new strategies to symbolize the meaning of statements such as the ones in this argument. In order to do this we will develop a system known as *predicate logic* (PL). In predicate logic we will include symbols for both predicates and the subjects and objects that accompany them. A predicate, for our purposes here, is the verb of the sentence.

Take for instance, the sentence "Bob dances." In PL, we could symbolize this statement like this:

Db

where *D* stands for the *predicate* "x dances" and *b* stands for the *subject*, "Bob."

In general we will use the symbolization *Px* to stand for some predicate or property *P* and some individual or thing, *x*, to which the predicate or property applies. If we have the predicate Dx, which stands for "x dances," we can symbolize various sentences for different individuals to which this predicate applies or doesn't apply. For instance,

Maria dances	Dm
Li doesn't dance	~Dl
Jean dances	Dj
etc.	

In this way we capture what is similar about the statements, as opposed to symbolizing these three statements as M, L, and J, respectively. Any statement can be symbolized in predicate notation. Here are some examples:

Bob sings	Sb	Sx = "x sings" b = "Bob"
Nathan runs every morning	Rn	Rx = "x runs every morning" n = "Nathan"
Fernando likes Bianca	Bf	Bx= "x likes Bianca." f = "Fernando"
Bianca likes Fernando	Fb	Fx = "x likes Fernando." Note that, like in SL, if *Bx* means "x likes Bianca," we have to use a different capital letter for "x likes Fernando."
Bianca likes Luis	Lb	Sx = "x likes Luis" Note that the subject in both of these last statements is Bianca, so x is replaced by "b" in both symbolizations.

Having translated statements into predicate form, we can do any of the logical operations that we have learned with the symbolizations. For instance, the normal translation rules apply:

Fernando likes Bianca, and Luis doesn't like Bianca

Bf & ~Bl

Fernando likes Bianca and Luis likes Bianca, and Bianca likes Fernando.

(Bf & Bl) & Fb

If Fernando likes Bianca, and Bianca doesn't like Fernando, then Luis likes Bianca if and only if Bianca likes Luis.

(Bf & ~Bb) → (Bl ≡ Lb)

5.2 – Multi-Place Predicates

The predicates we have considered so far are called *single-place* predicates because they involve only a predicate and a subject. However, in PL we can symbolize objects as well as subjects. For instance, the sentence "Fernando likes Bianca" contains a subject (Fernando), the predicate (likes) and an object (Bianca). It could be symbolized with this predicate:

Lfb

which is an instance of the general predicate,

Lxy

which means, "x likes y." This is called a *two-place* predicate, because there is a variable for both the subject and the object. Using multi-place predicates is very useful in capturing complex relationships among things. For instance, the statements we have already encountered about the relationships among Fernando, Luis, and Bianca can all be symbolized (and more easily) using this two-place predicate:

Fernando likes Bianca, and Luis doesn't like Bianca

Lfb & ~Llb

Fernando likes Bianca and Luis likes Bianca, and Bianca likes Fernando.

(Lfb & Llb) & Lbf

If Fernando likes Bianca, and Bianca doesn't like Fernando, then Luis likes Bianca if and only if Bianca likes Luis.

(Lfb & ~Lbf) → (Llb ≡ Lbl)

Any statement that has both a subject and an object can be symbolized with a two-place predicate. For instance:

Bob drives the car	Dbc	Dxy = "x drives y"
Li sings in the shower	Sls	Sxy = "x sings in y"
Millie wears the red hat	Wmh	Wxy = "x wears y"

It is possible to have predicates with even more than two variables. For instance:

San Francisco is between Los Angeles and Portland	Bslp	Bxyz = "x is between y and z"
Bob gives the gift to Jean	Gbgj	Gxyz = "x gives y to z"

Theoretically, there is no limit to how many variables a predicate can have, although there are practical limits to constructing statements with a great number of objects.

One general note about predicate logic is that *capital* letters symbolize predicates (verbs); while small letters from a through v symbolize *individual things* (people, places, things, etc.), which are nouns or noun phrases, and small letters from w through z are reserved for variables.

Exercises

Using the following predicate symbols and individuals, translate the sentences:

Lxy = x likes y
Fxy = x is from y
Dx = x dances
Wxy = x sings with y
Sx = x sings
a = Albert
b = Bob
c = Carmelia
d = Dora
l = Los Angeles
m = Memphis

Translate:

1. Albert sings and Albert dances, but Albert is not from Memphis.
2. If Albert sings with Carmelia, then Albert does not sing with Bob and Bob does not sing with Carmelia.
3. If Bob is from Los Angeles, then Caremelia likes him, but if Bob is from Memphis, then Carmelia doesn't like him.
4. Dora is from Memphis and she sings and dances, but neither Albert nor Bob like her.
5. Albert sings with Dora and Bob sings with Carmelia, but Albert doesn't sing with both Bob and Carmelia.
6. Albert, Dora, and Bob are all from Los Angeles, but Carmelia is from Memphis.
7. Either Albert is from Los Angeles and sings and dances, or Dora is from Memphis and doesn't sing or doesn't dance.
8. One of the four people is from Los Angeles.
9. All of the four people are from Memphis.
10. The four people are not all from Los Angeles, and none of the four people is from Memphis.

Chapter 6: Quantifier Logic: Translations

The last few exercises in chapter 5 introduce some ideas that lead into the next (and final) system of logic that we will discuss. The first is that if we are discussing a specific group of individuals, we can use the words "all," "no" or "none," or "some" to refer to the members of the group. The second is that, in doing PL symbolizations with the members of groups, if the group being discussed is very large, the symbolization will become very complex very quickly. Consider again the last exercise:

The four people are not all from Los Angeles, and none of the four people is from Memphis.

which we symbolized as:

~(Fal & (Fbl & (Fcl & Fdl))) & ~(Fam ∨ (Fbm ∨ (Fcm ∨ Fdm)))

This symbolization is already fairly complex. But what is we had a group of 100 people and we wanted to symbolize that they're not all from Los Angeles, and none of them are from Memphis? This would require a long and complex symbolization!

Quantifier Logic (QL) is an extension of Predicate Logic, and introduces some new symbols to help refer to predicates that apply to some, all or no members of a group.

6.1 – Universal Quantification

A statement that refers to ALL of the member of a group is symbolized like this:

AxPx

A capital A followed by a lowercase x is the logical quantification symbol for "All."[19] A statement of this form is read,

"for every x (in the specified group), x is (has the predicate) P"

or, more intuitively, "All x's are P."

---

[19] Some logic texts and websites use an upside-down A or (x) to represent "all."

6.2 – Particular or Existential Quantification

A statement that refers to SOME of the members of a group is symbolized like this:

ExPx

A capital E followed by a lowercase x is the logical symbolization for "Some"[20] (it is based on the logical idea that "some" means "there Exists at least one"). This statement reads,

"There is an x (in the specified group) that is (has the predicate) P"

or, more intuitively, "Some x's are P."

It is important to note that "some" in logic means no more than "at least one." We cannot determine from a particular or existential statement *how many* of a specified group have the property in question. It may be only one, it may be half the group, it may be all of the group except one, and, in fact, it may be the whole group. All we can determine from a particular statement is that AT LEAST ONE member of the group has the property, no more.

6.3 – Universe of Discourse

We have used the expression "in the specified group" several times. In quantifier logic, unless a particular group is specified, the group of things being considered is the whole universe. So, if we want to say something about human beings, it is easier to specify that this is the set of things we are considering. A set, so specified, is referred to as the "universe of discourse" (UD) for the statement(s). So, for instance, consider this universe of discourse and some possible predicates:

UD: Humans

Bx   =   x is bald

Now consider the following statement:

Some people are bald

---

[20] Some logic texts and websites use a backwards E or ($x) to represent "some."

This statement is a particular statement. It would be symbolized as

ExBx

This reads, "there is at least one member of the universe of discourse that is B(bald)." Note that in a quantified statement, we do not replace the variable x with any particular letter. We are symbolizing the fact that at least one person (identified by a variable, x) is bald, but we are not identifying any *particular* individuals as being the person who is bald. If we knew a person, Bob, who was bald, we could symbolize this as:

Bb

But since this is saying "Bob is bald," it is not a quantified sentence.

Suppose we wanted to symbolize (falsely), "All people are bald." It would be

AxBx

This reads, literally, "For every x (in the universe of discourse), x is bald." More naturally, it reads, "All the members of the universe of discourse are B(ald)."

Similarly, if we had the predicate

Hx = x has a heart

we could symbolize the statement, "All people have hearts" as

AxHx

which would read "All the members of the UD have hearts."

6.4 – Negated Quantified Statements

Given our universe of discourse (people) and our predicate, Bx, how might we symbolize

Not all people are bald

The easiest way to symbolize this statement is to view it as this:

NOT (All people are bald)

Now it is the negation of a universal statement, so we could just symbolize it as such:

~AxBx

This reads "It is not the case that all people are bald."

However, there is a different way to symbolize this statement as well. Given that not all people are bald, what would we know about people who are NOT bald? We would know that SOME people are NOT bald. This is a particular statement with a negated predicate:

Ex~Bx

This statement reads, "There is at least one person who is not bald," which has the same meaning as "not all people are bald."
Thus we have this equivalence rule for QL:

~AxPx ≡ Ex~Px

This can be read as "'it is not the case that all x's are P' iff (means the same thing as) 'there are some x's that are not P'"
Now consider the predicate Gx, meaning "x has gills." We can symbolize "No humans have gills" as

~ExGx

which would read, "it is not the case that there are some humans that have gills." Similarly, we could translate it as

Ax~Gx

which would read "All humans are such that they do not have gills," which means the same thing. So this equivalency exists as well:

~ExPx ≡ Ax~Px

Or, "'It is not the case that there are any x's that are P' iff 'All x's are such that they are not P.'"

6.5 – Quantification Without a Universe of Discourse

Suppose we had the predicate Gx, (x has gills), but did not specify a universe of discourse. Then this statement:

Ax~Gx

would read, "for every x (in the universe), x doesn't have gills." But this is false, because some things in the universe have gills. We can specify particular groups of things by including more predicates in our symbolization scheme. For instance, consider this set:

Fx = x is a fish
Hx = x is a human
Gx = x has gills
Lx = x has lungs

With these additional predicates, we can symbolize complex relationships among groups of things without specifying a universe of discourse (which means that the universe of discourse is the whole universe):

(All) Fish have gills.

This statement means that anything that is a fish has gills, or, *if* something is a fish, *then* it has gills. This condition applies to all things in the universe. So we can symbolize it:

Ax(Fx → Gx)

"For every x, if x is a fish, then x has gills."

Similarly, "No people have gills" would mean that if something is a person, it doesn't have gills. So:

Ax(Hx → ~Gx)

If we wanted to symbolize "(All) Fish have gills and (all) people have lungs," it would be:

Ax(Fx → Gx) & Ax(Hx → Lx)

Now let us go back to our earlier predicate, Bx (x is bald). If we wanted to symbolize "some people are bald", with no universe of discourse specified, it would be:

Ex(Px & Bx)

"There is an x such that x is a person and x is bald."

Similarly, "Some people are not bald" would be

Ex(Px & ~Bx)

"There is an x such that x is a person and x is not bald."

Note the different forms that a universal statement and a particular statement have. Universals without a specified UD take the form of a conditional: "All Ps are Qs" becomes "for every x, *if* x is a P, *then* x is a Q." Particular statements without a specified UD take the form of a conjunction: "Some Ps are Qs" becomes "there is an x such that x is a P and x is a Q." These patterns are very helpful to remember when doing more complex symbolizations.

6.6 – Quantification with Multi-place Predicates

Next, suppose we had the following UD and predicates:

UD: Humans

Mx = x has a mother
Fxy = x is y's father
Cxy = x is y's child

Symbolizing "everyone has a mother" would be fairly easy; it would just be "For all x's, x has a mother." So:

AxMx

Now suppose we wanted to symbolize, "everyone has a father." Our predicate here is Fxy, which means "x is y's father." We need a quantifier for both the subject (x, the father) and the object (y, the child), and we want to symbolize that for all people (x), there is someone (y) who is their father. We could symbolize this as:

AxEyFyx

This statement reads, "for every x (person) there is a y (person) such that person y is person x's father." Note that the order of the x and the y as quantified is different than their order in the blank predicate. This is necessary. Consider the following statement, which has the x and the y in the other order in the predicate:

AxEyFxy

This statement reads, "for every x (person) there is a y (person) such that person x is (person) y's father." This means, "everyone is the father of someone." This is clearly not the same statement and is clearly untrue. The order of the quantifiers also affects the meaning of the statement. Consider the original statement with the quantifiers reversed:

EyAxFyx

This statement reads, "there is a y (person) such that for all x's (people), y is x's father." But this means, "some one individual is the father of everyone." Again, this statement means something different and is untrue.

Now suppose we had the statement, "Everyone is someone's child." Our predicate here is Cxy, which means, "x is y's child." Again, we need quantifiers for both x and y. *x* refers to all members of the group, so we will use a universal quantifier for it. But *y* only refers to some particular individual(s) in the group, so we will use an existential quantifier for it. Our statement will look like this:

AxEyCxy

This statement reads, "For every x (person) there is a y (person) such that person x is person y's child." Or, back into normal English, "everyone is the child of someone." The order of the quantifiers again affects the meaning (and truth of the statement). Consider this statement with the quantifiers in the other order:

EyAxCxy

This statement reads, "there is a y (person) such that for *every* x (person), x is person y's child." This means that there is an individual who is the parent of everyone! The order of the *variables* in the predicate also, again, affects the meaning of the statement. If we switched the order of the variables in the predicate, we would get:

AxEyCyx

This statement reads, "for all x's (people) there is a y (person) such that y is x's child." This means that all people have children, which, again, is untrue.

As we saw with predicate logic, we can have compound statements with quantifiers. Consider,

Everyone has a father, but not everyone has a child.

Quantificationally, this would be "for all w's there is an x such that x is w's father, but it is not the case that for all y's there is a z such that z is y's child." The symbolization would be:

AwExFxw & ~AyEzCzy

Consider,

Some people have children, but it is not the case that all people have children

Quantificationally, this would be, "for some w's there is an x such that w is x's child, and NOT(for all y's there is a z such that z is y's child)."

EwExCwx & ~AyEzCzy

6.7 – Quantification with Multiple Quantifiers, Multi-place Predicates and Expanded UDs

As we noted with single-place predicates, sometimes we have multi-place predicates and a large (or no) specified universe of discourse. The symbolizations for these statements can become very complex, so it is helpful to begin with some simpler ones to see the form.

Consider the predicate, Lxy, x likes y, and a UD of "people." Now consider the following statements:

1.   Everyone likes everyone.
2.   Everyone likes someone.
3.   Someone likes everyone.
4.   Someone likes someone.

The symbolizations would be:

1.   AxAyLxy
"For all x's and all y's, x likes y."

2.   AxEyLxy
"For all x's there is a y such that x likes y."

3.   ExAyLxy
"There is an x such that for all y's, x likes y."

4.   ExEyLxy
"There is an x and a y such that x likes y"

Now consider the same statements, but without a UD:

1.   AxAy(Px → (Py → Lxy))
"For all x's and all y's, IF x is a person, THEN, if y is a person, then x likes y."[21]

2.   AxEy(Px → (Py & Lxy))
"For all x's there is a y such that IF x is a person, then y IS a person and x likes y."

3.   ExAy(Px & (Py → Lxy))

---

[21] Intuitively, it seems that this statement could be translated as $(\forall x)(\forall y)((Px \& Py) \to Lxy)$, "For all x's and all y's, if x is a person and y is a person, then x likes y." In fact, this is an equivalent translation. Remember the replacement rule of exportation: $(p \to (q \to r)) \equiv ((p \& q) \to r)$. This translation is an instance of this replacement rule.

"There is an x such that for every y, x IS a person and IF y is a person, then x likes y."

4.   ExEy(Px & (Py & Lxy))
"There is an x and a y such that x is a person and y is a person, and x likes y."

The thing to note about multiple quantifiers with no UD is the form the symbolization take. The easiest way to remember this is to think of nested parentheses. The outside parenthesis will take the form of the first quantifier (a conditional for a universal and a conjunction for a particular) and the inside parentheses will take the form of the second quantifier (a conditional for a universal and a conjunction for a particular). Review each of the four symbolizations above to see this pattern. As symbolizations become more complex, remembering this pattern will make the symbolizations much easier.

Consider some more complex statements like our earlier ones about cars and bikes, with no specified UD:

1.   Everyone owns a car.
2.   Everyone owns a car, and not everyone drives a car.
3.   Some people drive a car, and some people ride a bike
4.   Some people drive a car and ride a bike.
5.   Some people own cars and don't drive them.
6.   Some people prefer their bike to their car.
7.   Everyone who owns a car drives their car.
8.   No one drives any car they don't own.
9.   Someone (some individual person) owns every car (all the cars in the world). (This statement is false!)

Now consider these predicates and no specified universe of discourse:

Px   = x is a person
Cx   = x is a car
Bx   = x is a bike
Oxy   = x owns y
Dxy   = x drives y
Rxy   = x rides y
Rxyz = x prefers y to z

The symbolizations of these sentences would be, respectively,

1. AxEy[Px → (Cy & Oxy)]

This reads, "for every x there is a y such that if x is a person then y is some car and x owns y." Since we are not working with a UD of just people, we have to specify which type of thing in the universe our x and y are in addition to specifying their relationships. Note again the form of the statement; a conditional in the outside parentheses, because the first quantifier is a universal, and a conjunction in the inside parentheses, because the second quantifier is a particular.

2. AxEy[Px → (Cy &Oxy)] & ~AxEy[Px → (Cy & Dxy)]

Note here that we used x and y in both statements. This is fine. You cannot use a variable for more than one type of individual in a single statement, but variables can be used to represent different things in different statements. After all, there are only 4 variables to use!

3. ExEy[(Px & Cy) & Dxy] & ExEy[(Px & By) & Rxy]

This reads, "there is an x and there is a y such that x is a person and y is a car and x (the person) drives y (the car) and there is an x and there is a y such that x is a person and y is a bike and x (the person) rides y (the bike)." Since both are particular, the quantified statements take the form of conjunctions.

4. ExEyEz[(Px & (Cy & Bz)) & (Dxy & Rxz)]

This reads, "there is an x and a y and a z such that x is a person and y is a car and z is a bike and x (the person) drives y (the car) and x rides z (the bike)." Since we have to have variables for a person, a car and a bike all in the same sentence, we have to use 3 quantifers (x, y, z).

5. ExEy[(Px & Cy) & (Oxy & ~Dxy)]

This reads, "there is an x and there is a y such that x is a person and y is a car and x (the person) owns y (the car) and/but x (the person) doesn't drive y (the car)."

6. ExEyEz[((Px & (Cy & Bz)) & (Oxy & Oxz)) & Rxzy]

This complicated statement reads, "there is an x and there is a y and there is a z such that x is a person and y is a car and z is a bike and x (the person) owns y (the car) and x owns z (the bike) and x prefers z (the bike) to y (the car)." This example is mainly to show a 3-place predicate, which requires three quantifiers. Since all the quantifiers are particular, the statement is a long conjunction.

7. AxAy[Px → ((Cy & Oxy) → Dxy)] OR
     AxAy[(Px & (Cy & Oxy)) → Dxy]

This is an example of the exportation equivalence rule. The first statement says, "for every x and every y, IF x is a person, THEN if y is a car and x (the person) owns y (the car), then x drives y." The second, equivalent statement, says, "for every x and every y, IF x is a person AND y is a car and x (the person) owns y (the car), THEN x drives y."

8. AxAy[Px → ((Cy & ~Oxy) → ~Dxy)] OR
     AxAy[(Px & (Cy & ~Oxy)) → ~Dxy]

First; "for every x and every y, IF x is a person, THEN if y is a car and x doesn't own y, then x doesn't drive y." Second; "for every x and every y, IF x is a person AND y is a car and x doesn't own y, then x doesn't drive y."

9. ExAy[(Px & (Cy → Oxy))

This reads, "there is an x such that for every y, x is a person and if y is a car, then x owns y." Since the first quantifier is particular, the outside parentheses are a conjunction. Since the second quantifier is universal, the inside parentheses are a conditional.

Exercises

Single-place predicates
Using the specified universe of discourse and predicates, translate the following statements into quantificational form (a number of these statements are false; don't worry about that at this point):

UD: Humans.

Mx = x has a mother
Sx = x has a sister
Bx = x has a brother

Cx = x has a child

1. Everyone has a mother.
2. Not everyone has a child.
3. Some people have sisters and some people have brothers.
4. Some people have children, but everyone has a mother.
5. Some people don't have a child, but it is not the case that some people don't have a mother.
6. If everyone has a child, then everyone has a sister.
7. If someone has a child, then someone has a mother.
8. Some people have both brothers and sisters.
9. Not everyone has a brother or a sister.
10. Not everyone has a brother and a sister.
11. Some people don't have a brother or a sister.
12. Some people have a mother, but no brother or sister.
13. Some people have a mother, and have a brother if and only if they have a sister.
14. Everyone has a child if and only if they have a mother, and if they have a sister, then they have a brother.

Multi-place predicates

Using the specified universe of discourse and predicates, translate the following statements into quantificational form (a number of these statements are false; don't worry about that at this point):

UD: Humans

Lxy = x likes y
Mxy = x misses y
Ox = x is out of town

1. Everyone likes someone.
2. Some people like some people.
3. No one likes everyone.
4. No one likes no one.
5. Some people like everyone.
6. Everyone likes and misses someone.
7. People miss other people if and only if they like them.
8. If anyone doesn't miss someone, then they don't like them.
9. If anyone likes anyone else, and the person they like is out of town, they miss them.

10. If anyone doesn't like someone, and the person they don't like is out of town, they don't miss them.

Multi-place predicates with expanded UD

Using the specified predicates, and no specified universe of discourse, translate the following statements into quantificational form.

Lxy	=	x likes y
Sxy	=	x sits on y's lap
Fxy	=	x licks y's face
Px	=	x is a person
Dx	=	x is a dog
Tx	=	x wags its tail
Mx	=	x is a male
Fx	=	x is a female

1. Everyone dislikes someone.
2. No person dislikes everyone.
3. No person likes everyone.
4. Some men like all women.
5. Some men like some women.
6. Some men don't like any women.
7. Some women like only women.
8. Some people like all dogs.
9. Some dogs don't like any people.
10. Some people don't like any dogs.
11. Some people like no people or dogs.
12. If a dog likes a person, it wags its tail, licks his/her face and sits on his/her lap.
13. All male dogs lick all female dogs' faces.

Chapter 7: Quantifier Logic: Derivations

7.1 – Quantifier Derivation Rules

One quick note to begin: we are returning now to the system of Natural Deduction (ND). All the replacement rules and inference rules, and conditional proof and indirect proof are in play once again. We will now add some rules to the ND system to deal with quantifiers. The quantification truth tree rules introduce the first set of quantification derivation rules. The first two are the negated quantifier rules, which we have dealt with.

~AE	~EE
~AxPx	~ExPx
→Ex~Px	→Ax~Px

The next two rules deal with existential statements. As in our earlier derivation rules, we need rules to derive statements *from* existential statements and to derive existential statements from other statements.

Existential Generalization (EG)

Pa*   *"a" can be any constant
→ ExPx

Existential generalization is the easiest of the quantifier rules. It says simply that if any particular thing has a property P, then you can immediately generalize to the claim that at least one thing has the property P. For instance, if Carlos is bald, then it follows that *someone* is bald.

Existential Instantiation (EI)

ExPx
→ Pa* (a/x),   *where "a" is a constant NOT USED anywhere
previously in the derivation.

To "instantiate" is to replace a quantified statement with a regular statement. We have to get rid of the quantifiers in order to do the logic with the statements. But we have to be careful what kind of a statement we turn quantified statements into, or the logic doesn't work. Existential instantiation, turning an existential statement into a regular statement, has an important limitation. It says that you can only instantiate an existential statement with some *unused* constant. That means, if the constant ("a" or whatever the letter

169.

we are using) has been used somewhere else in the proof for some other statement, and cannot be used to instantiate an existential. The existential instantiation must use a *unique* constant. We will see examples of why this is important after learning the rules.

Universal Instantiation (AI)

Universal derivation rules are among the trickiest of all logical rules. Universal Instantiation is this:

AxPx
→ Pa*, (*a/x*)   * *"a" can be any letter at all*

The use of "a" in a universal instantiation is peculiar. It is referred to as a "non-specified constant." Think of it as a *quasi-variable*. That is, "a" doesn't stand for some particular individual, but some randomly selected, non-specified individual. Since Px holds for all individuals, it will hold for any particular individual. This idea must be remembered when working with Universal Generalization, which we will discuss next.

Universal Generalization (AG)

Pa*
→ AxPx   **provided that "a" entered the proof as a non-specified constant (through AI) and NOT as a specified constant (through EI) or an individual constant (through given statements)*

This rule says that if you have a statement Pa, in which the "a" has been introduced as a non-specified constant or a quasi-variable, through a universal instantiation, then you can generalize from Pa to the universal statement, AxPx. In short, this means that "a" *must have been introduced by a AI and not by an EI.* If "a" had been introduced from an EI, we would only know that the predicate holds for some specific individual(s); we wouldn't know that it holds for any random individual in the UD. We will see examples of why this holds.

7.2 – Quantifier Derivation Strategies

Quantificational derivations can be tricky. The trickiest part of quantificational derivations is AG. Small-case letters can stand for three different things: individuals (like Albert), specific constants (in the case of EI), or non-specific constants (in the case of AI). The meaning of a small-case letter thus must be tracked carefully through a proof. Here are some examples:

UD: people
Bx: x is bald
Tx: x wears a hat
Hx: x has a heart
Vx: x has blood vessels
a: Albert

Ba
∴ ***AxBx**

This argument reads, "Albert is bald, therefore everyone is bald." This is clearly invalid. Without the limitation on AG, we might get this:

1.	Ba	Given
2.	*AxBx	*1, AG. This is an incorrect use of AG. "a" has been introduced as an individual constant, Albert, not as a non-specific constant (any random individual in the UD.) So we cannot generalize from Ba to AxBx in this case.

ExBx
∴ ***AxBx**

This argument reads, "someone is bald, therefore, everyone is bald." This is clearly invalid. Without the limitation on AG, we might get this:

1.	ExBx	Given
2.	Bb	1, EI Note that we didn't use "a", because "a" has been specified as "Albert" in our UD and we don't know that Albert is bald. "b"

171.

stands for some specific individual who is bald (even though we don't know who it is).[22]

3.　　　*AxBx　　*2, AG　This is an incorrect use of AG. "b" has been introduced as a specific constant (some individual who is bald), but not as a non-specific constant (any random individual in the UD.) So we cannot generalize from Bb to AxBx in this case.

Ax(Hx → Vx)

AxHx

∴AxVx

This argument says, "Everyone who has a heart has blood vessels; everyone has a heart, so everyone has blood vessels." The proof would be:

1. Ax(Hx → Vx)　　Given
2. AxHx　　　　　　Given
3. Hb → Vb　　1, AI　We are now using "b" as a non-specific constant. It stands for "any randomly selected member of the UD" – not an individual like Albert or a specific constant (like the person who is bald).

4. Hb　　　　　2, AI　Since Hx refers to all the members of the UD, we can use "b" for it (and for as many universal instantiations as we want) in the same proof.

5. Vb　　　　　3,4, MP　Once we have instantiated the universals, the normal derivation rules apply.

6. AxVx　　5, AG　Since the "b" in line 5 is a non-specific constant (it stands for any randomly selected individual), we can generalize

---

[22] Note: some logic texts require introducing an existential generalization as an added assumption in a subproof to protect against the possibility of trying to generalize it to a universal. So long as we keep careful track of how constants have been introduced, we can work without this added complexity.

from it to AxVx, according to AG. The key here is that "b" entered the proof from a AI. The general rule is that only constants that enter the proof from AI can be used for AG.

Ax(Bx → Tx)
Ba
∴ Ta

This argument says, "Anyone who is bald wears a hat. Albert is bald, so Albert wears a hat. ." (We are interested in validity here, not soundness, so the truth of the first premise is immaterial). The proof would be:

1.	Ax(Bx → Tx)	Given	
2.	Ba	Given	
3.	Ba → Ta	1, AI.	There are no limits on instantiating a universal. We can use any letter we want, since the predicate applies to all the members of the UD. So it would have to apply to Albert. But note: we could NOT do a AG on any further result from this instantiation, because "a" is not a non-specific constant, it is an individual.
4.	Ta	2,3,MP	The normal derivation rules apply. This is the end of the proof. But we can look at some more possibilities.
5.	ExTx	4, EG	This is a valid move. We have shown that Albert wears a hat, so at least one member of the UD wears a hat. The proof didn't require this move, but it's valid.
6.	*AxTx	*4, AG	This is an invalid move. All we've shown in our proof is that one individual ("a") wears a hat. We

cannot generalize from this fact to
the claim that ALL the members
wear hats. Since "a" entered the
proof as an individual constant, we
cannot generalize from it to a
universal.

Ax(Bx → Tx)

ExBx

∴ExTx

This argument says "Anyone who is bald wears a hat. Some people
are bald. Therefore, some people wear hats. The proof would be:

1. **Ax(Bx → Tx)** Given

2. **ExBx**   Given

3. **Bb**   2, **EI**   As an we instantiate the
                                     existential first, because it
                                     has to be instantiated with a
                                     letter that doesn't appear
                                     elsewhere. We can't use a,
                                     because we don't know in
                                     this case whether Albert is
                                     bald.

4. **Bb → Tb**   1, **AI.** There are no limits on
                                     instantiating a universal. We
                                     can use any letter we want,
                                     since the predicate applies to
                                     all the members of the UD.
                                     So it would have to apply to
                                     whichever individual "b"
                                     specifies. But note: we
                                     could NOT do a **AG** on any
                                     further result from this
                                     instantiation, because "b" is
                                     not a non-specific constant,
                                     but a specific constant.

5. **Tb**   3,4,MP Again, the normal derivation
                                     rules apply.

6. **ExTx**   5, **EG**   The rule of EG says that

from any statement Pa, we can generalize to an existential, since Pa just says that some individual (a) is a P. In this case we have derived that some individual (b) is T. Since at least one individual is T, we can assert ExTx. This is the end of the proof

7.   *AxTx   *5, AG This is an invalid move. "b" was introduced as a specific constant (line 3), not a non-specific constant. All we know in this proof is that some individual (b) is T, not that ALL (i.e., randomly selected) b's are T.

7.3 – Derivations With Multiple Quantifiers

Although they become increasingly complex, derivations with multiple quantifiers don't involve any new or different rules. Here are some examples:

UD: People
Lxy: x likes y
b: Bob
m: Marie

Lbm
∴ExEyLxy

This says, "Bob likes Marie, so someone likes someone." The proof is:

1.   Lbm   Given
2.   ExLxm   1, EG   We do an existential generalization on one of the constants. We end up with "someone likes Marie" (the order of doing this doesn't matter).

175.

3. ExEyLxy   2, EG   We do an existential generalization on the other constant, using a different variable. We now have, "Someone likes someone."

AxAyLxy
∴ExEyLxy

This says, "everyone likes everyone, so someone likes someone."

1. AxAyLxy   Given
2. AyLay   1, AI   We do a universal instantiation on one of the universals in the premise (it doesn't matter which you start with). The other universal remains part of the statement.
3. Lab   2, AI   We do a universal instantiation on the other universal. We use a different letter for this instantiation.
4. ExLxb   3, EG   Now we do an existential generalization on one of the constants (again, it doesn't matter which we do first). Since we know that there's some individual that likes, we can do the generalization.
5. ExEyLxy   2, EG   Now we do an existential generalization on the other constant.

UD: Everything
Hxy: x hunts y
Lx: x is a lion
Zx: x is a zebra

AxAy((Lx & Zy) → Hxy)
ExLx
ExZx
∴ExEyHxy

This says, "Every lion hunts every zebra. There are lions. There are zebras. Therefore, there are some things that hunt other things.

1.	$AxAy((Lx \& Zy) \rightarrow Hxy)$	Given	
2.	$ExLx$	Given	
3.	$ExZx$	Given	
4.	La	2, EI	We instantiate the first existential with a letter.
5.	Zb	3, EI	We instantiate the second existential with a different letter.
6.	$Ax((Lx \& Zb) \rightarrow Hxb)$	1, AI	We instantiate one of the two universal quantifiers in the first statement, using the letter that we used to apply to that predicate – in this case we instantiated Ay with "b".
7.	$(La \& Zb) \rightarrow Hab$	1, AI	We instantiate the other universal quantifier with the letter that gives us the result we need – in this case we instantiate Ax with "a". The order of the instantiation if the multi-place statement is all universals or all existentials doesn't matter.
8.	$La \& Zb$	4,5, &I	Normal derivation rules apply.
9.	Hab	7,8, MP	Normal derivation rule.
10.	$ExHxb$	9, EG	We can generalize from any statement to the existential.

But we have to do it in steps. We first generalize from a to x (the order doesn't matter).

11. ExEyHxy   10, EG   We generalize from b to y.

Exercises

Translate the following arguments, if necessary, and derive the conclusions.

UD: Everything
Ax: x is an animal
Bx: x is bald
Cx: x is a cat
Hx: x is 100 feet tall
Lx: x has lungs
Px: x is a person
f: Francois

A. All people have lungs. Francois is a person. Therefore, Francois has lungs.
B. No people are 100 feet tall. Francois is a person. Therefore, Francois is not 100 feet tall.
C. All animals have lungs. All cats are animals. Therefore, all cats have lungs.
D. All people have lungs. Some people are bald. Therefore, some bald things either have lungs or wings.

UD: People
Dx: x is a Democrat
Hx: x is honest
Mx: x is from Mississippi
Px: x is a politician
Tx: x is from Texas
f: Francois

E. All politicians are dishonest. Some politicians are from Mississippi. Therefore, some Mississippians are dishonest.
F. No one from Texas or Mississippi is honest. Some politicians are from Mississippi. Therefore, some politicians are dishonest.

G. Francois is either a Texan or a politician. Francois is bald. All Texans are dishonest. All politicians are dishonest. Therefore, there are some dishonest bald people.

H. $AxAy((Bx \lor Cy) \rightarrow Axy)$
   $AxCx$ $\therefore AxAyAxy$

I. $AxEy(Az)(Dx \rightarrow ((Fy \lor Gz) \rightarrow Jxyz))$
   $Ex(Dx \,\&\, Gx)$ $\therefore Ex(Jxax)$

J. $AxAy((Nx \lor My) \rightarrow Oxy)$
   $Ew(Az)(Nw \,\&\, (Pz \rightarrow Lwz))$
   $AwPw$ $\therefore ExEy(Oyx \,\&\, Lyx)$

Chapter 8: Quantifier Logic: Truth Trees

8.1 – Quantifier Truth Tree Rules

The truth tree rules we learned earlier all apply to statements and arguments that involve quantifiers. However, we must add some rules to work with quantifiers in truth trees. The first two we have already learned; they are the rules for moving negations from outside of quantifiers to inside of quantifiers:

Negated Quantifier Rules

$$\underline{\sim\text{AD}}$$
$$\sim\text{AxPx}$$
$$|$$
$$\text{Ex}\sim\text{Px}$$

$$\underline{\sim\text{ED}}$$
$$\sim\text{ExPx}$$
$$|$$
$$\text{Ax}\sim\text{Px}$$

With these rules we can change any negated quantified statement into a non-negated quantified statement. Now we need some rules for dealing with non-negated quantified statements. We will start with the easier of the two:

Universal Instantiation (AI)

$$\underline{\text{AI}}$$
$$\text{AxPx}$$
$$|$$
$$\text{Pa } (a/x)$$

This rule states we can replace a universally quantified statement, AxPx, with the statement, Pa, where a is a *substitution instance* for x. A substitution instance is an individual that replaces a variable. Since the universally quantified statement claims that the property P applies to ALL individuals in the universe of discourse, *any* individual from the universe will have the property P. "a" in this case stands for some randomly selected individual, so Pa must be true, since all individuals have/are P. In the case of universal statements, we say that "a" is a *quasi-variable*. That is, while "a" stands for an individual, it is being used to represent "some randomly selected individual", not some specific individual. So it is somewhere between being an individual and a variable. Note that the rule is called "Universal Instantiation," not "Universal Elimination." Universal statements are unique in that they are not eliminated – a universal statement may be instantiated in a proof as many times as desired or required. Note also that in doing a universal instantiation, the instantiation line need not include the "(a/x)"; it only needs the "Pa."

Existential Instantiation (EI)

ExPx

|

Pa (*a/x*), where "a" is a letter NOT USED anywhere previously in the tree.

Existential instantiation is more complicated. The complication is that an existential statement asserts that *some* individual in the UD has property P, but it doesn't specify anything about *which* individual has it. This means that we have to be careful when we instantiate the existential, so we don't assert more than we know.

To illustrate, consider this case. Suppose we have the following model:

UD: People
Bx: x is bald
a: Albert

Now suppose we have the following argument:

Some people are bald, therefore, Albert is bald.

And the following symbolization:

ExBx   / ∴ Ba

Intuitively, this argument is invalid. We cannot infer from the premise that some people are bald, the conclusion that Albert is bald, because he may not be part of the subset of people who are bald. Now consider this truth-tree proof for this argument:

1.	ExBx	Given
2.	~Ba	Given/Assumed
3.	*Ba	*1, EI
	X	

This truth tree closes. Remember, to test an argument with a truth tree, you complete a tree of the argument combined with the *negation of the conclusion*. If the tree closes, the argument plus the negation of the conclusion is inconsistent, which means that it is not possible for all the premises and the negation of the conclusion to be true, which means that is not possible for the premises to be true and the (non-negated) conclusion to be false, which means that the argument is *valid*. So this argument comes out valid, while intuitively we saw that it should be invalid.

The error in this proof arises from instantiating an existential statement with an individual constant that had already appeared in the proof (in this case in the negated conclusion). This asserts that the predicate B holds for the already-named individual "a." But this asserts too much. Again, we know that some person or people are bald, but that information does not warrant the inference that Albert, the specific individual, is bald. This is why the existential instantiation rule includes the caveat that the quasi-variable chosen for the instantiation MUST NOT have appeared earlier in the proof. It must be a quasi-variable that has never appeared. This asserts that there is some individual to whom the property applies, but that we do not know who it is, and that we do not know that it applies to any individual already identified in the proof.

Now consider this argument completed correctly.

1. ExBx   Given
2. ~Ba   Given/Assumed
3. Bb   1, EI

In this case, at line 3, we instantiated the existential statement with a quasi-variable different from "a". It doesn't matter which letter of the alphabet is used, so long as it has not been used before. Since ~Ba and Bb do not mean the same thing, there is no contradiction between them. Thus, the tree is open, so it is possible for the premises and the negation of the conclusion all to be true, so it is possible for the premises to be true while the conclusion is false, so the argument is invalid. Now it matches our intuitive understanding of it.

8.2 Truth Tree Proofs

We are now prepared to complete truth tree proofs involving quantifiers. The only properties we will consider here are consistency and validity. Consistency is the easiest property to test: a set of statements is consistent if and only if it has an open truth three (at least one open branch). Consider this model and set of statements:

UD: people
Bx: x is bald
Mx: x is a man.
Wx: x is a weightlifter

All bald people are men.
Some people are bald.
Some people are not men.

Ax(Bx → Mx)

ExBx

Ex~Mx

To test this set for consistency, we just do a truth tree for it.

1.	Ax(Bx → Mx)	Given
2.	ExBx	Given
3.	Ex~Mx	Given

Strategy is important in quantifier truth trees. We know we can instantiate a universal statement to ANY quasi-variable, because we know that the properties must apply to ALL the members of the UD. And we know that we CANNOT instantiate an existential to any previously used quasi-variable. So if we instantiate the particular statements first, we can use those same letters to instantiate the universal, because universal instantiation doesn't have the same limitation as existential instantiation.

1.	Ax(Bx → Mx)	Given
2.	ExBx	Given
3.	Ex~Mx	Given
4.	Ba	2, EI
5.	~Mb	3, EI

Notice here that on line 4, we instantiated line 3 with an "a" and on line 5 we instantiated line 3 with a "b." This is necessary by the EI rule – we have to instantiate each different existential claim with a different letter. Now we can instantiate the universal statement. A question now arises: we have to individual letters, "a" and "b." Which should we use? The first answer is, the goal of truth trees is to close branches. If you can instantiate the universal statement in a way that closes one or more branches, do it. The second answer is, a universal statement can be instantiated as many times as you want or need. Before you are done, you must instantiate it for each letter on the branch beneath it. In this case, we have two; a and b.

1.	Ax(Bx → Mx)	Given
2.	ExBx	Given
3.	Ex~Mx	Given
4.	Ba	2, EI
5.	~Mb	3, EI
6.	Ba → Ma	1, AI

7.　~Ba　　　　　　Ma　　6, → E
　　　✗

Here we have instantiated the universal with "a" and the left branch closes. The right branch contains a ~Mb and an Ma. But these are not contradictory, since they apply to different individuals. So this branch does not close. Since there is still another letter on the branch under the universal statement (b), we have to instantiate it again for that letter.

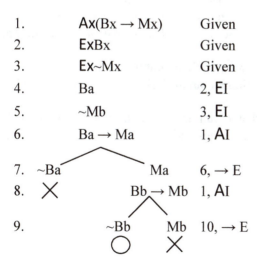

Our truth tree has one open branch. This means that the set of statements is consistent. This set of statements again illustrates the limited knowledge that can be inferred from existential statements. The first statement says that all Fs are Bs. The second statement says that there is one

F that is a C. The third statement says there is something that is not a B. Intuitively, it seems that since all Fs are Bs (from line 1), and something is an F (from line 2), that thing must be a B (since ALL Fs are Bs). And this is correct. It then might seem that it would necessarily be false that something could be a non-B (i.e., line 3 must be false). But this does not follow. The universal statement does not claim that everything in the UD IS an F, just that IF anything is an F, it is also a B. So the fact that one thing is an F and a B does not mean that there are not things that are not Bs – anything that is not an F may not be a B. So it is consistent to assert that some things are neither Fs nor Bs.

Exercises

Part 1: Translate the following sets of statements and use truth trees to test them for consistency.

UD: Everything
Ax: x is an animal
Bx: x is bald
Lx: x has lungs
Px: x is a person
Wx: x has wings

A. Some people are bald. Some people are not bald.
B. Some animals have lungs. Some animals do not have lungs.
C. Some animals have lungs. Some animals have wings. Some animals are bald.
D. All people have lungs. Some people do not have lungs.
E. All animals have lungs. Some animals have wings. Some animals don't have wings.
F. It is not the case either that all animals have lungs or that all animals have wings. Some animals have wings and lungs. Some animals have neither wings nor lungs.

For the following problems, use this model:

UD: People
Cx: x is a politician
Dx: x is a Democrat
Hx: x is honest
Mx: x is from Mississippi
Tx: x is from Texas
f: Francois

A. All politicians are dishonest. All Mississippians are honest. Some politicians are from Mississippi. (NOTE: you don't have to include the predicate "x is a person" in the translations)
B. Some Democratic politicians are Mississippians. Some Democratic politicians are dishonest. No Mississippians are dishonest. (Don't include "x is a person" in the translations)
C. Francois is either a Texan or a Mississippian. Francois is a politician. Francois is bald. All Texans are dishonest. All politicians are dishonest. There are no dishonest bald people. (Don't include "x is a person" in the translations)
D. If some Texans are not politicians, then all Texans are honest. If some dishonest people are from Mississippi, then no politicians are from Mississippi. Some dishonest people are from Mississippi. (Don't include "x is a person" in the translations).

Part 2: Translate the following arguments and use truth trees to test them for validity (the question of soundness (the truth of the premises) is not at issue here; only the question of validity).

UD: Everything
Ax: x is an animal
Bx: x is bald
Lx: x has lungs
Px: x is a person
Wx: x has wings
f: Francois

A. All people have lungs. Francois is a person. Therefore, Francois has lungs.
B. All people have lungs. Francois has lungs. Therefore, Francois is a person.
C. Some animals have wings. Some animals have lungs. Therefore, some animals have both wings and lungs.
D. All animals have lungs. All animals have wings. Therefore, all animals have wings and lungs.

UD: People
Cx: x is a politician
Dx: x is a Democrat
Hx: x is honest
Mx: x is from Mississippi
Tx: x is from Texas

f: Francois

E. All politicians are dishonest. Some politicians are from Mississippi. Therefore, some Mississippians are dishonest.
F. Some politicians are dishonest. Some Mississippians are politicians. Therefore, some Mississippians are dishonest.
G. No one from Texas or Mississippi is honest. Some dishonest politicians are from Mississippi. Therefore, no Texans are politicians.
H. Some Texan politicians are honest. No honest politicians are from Mississippi. Some honest people are from neither Texas nor Mississippi. Therefore, some politicians are not from either Texas or Mississippi.
I. Francois is either a Texan or a Mississippian. Francois is a politician. Francois is bald. All Texans are dishonest. All politicians are dishonest. Therefore, there are some dishonest bald people.
J. If some Texans are not politicians, then all Texans are honest. If some dishonest people are from Mississippi, then no politicians are from Mississippi. Therefore, some dishonest people are not from Mississippi.

CPSIA information can be obtained
at www.ICGtesting.com
Printed in the USA
LVHW050000240122
709154LV00017B/2766